Turkish Coast

HarperCollins*Publishers*

This book was produced using QuarkXPress™ and
Adobe Illustrator 88™ on Apple Macintosh™ computers
and output to separated film on a Linotronic™ 300 Imagesetter

Text: Neil Wilson
Photography: T. F. Larsen-Collinge ABIPP
Cartography: Susan Harvey Design
Design: Lynsey Roxburgh

First published 1991
Copyright © HarperCollins Publishers
Produced by Collins Manufacturing, Glasgow
ISBN 0 00 435762 0

HOW TO USE THIS BOOK

Your Collins Traveller Guide will help you find your way around your holiday destination quickly and easily. It is split into two sections which are colour-coded:

The blue section provides you with an alphabetical sequence of headings, from **ANCIENT SITES** to **WALKS** via **EXCURSIONS**, **RESTAURANTS**, **SHOPPING**, etc. Each entry within a topic includes information on how to get there, how much it will cost you, when it will be open and what to expect. Furthermore, every page has its own map showing the position of each item and the nearest landmark. This allows you to orientate yourself quickly and easily in your new surroundings. To find what you want to do – having dinner, visiting a museum, going for a walk or shopping for gifts – simply flick through the blue headings and take your pick!

The red section is an alphabetical list of information. It provides essential facts about places and cultural items – 'What is a Dolmuş?', 'When is the Camel-wrestling Festival?', 'Where is Ephesus?' – and expands on subjects touched on in the first half of the book. This section also contains practical travel information. It ranges through how to find accommodation, where to hire a car, the variety of eating places and food available, tips on health, information on money, which newspapers are available, how to find a taxi and where the Youth Hostels are. It is lively and informative and easy to use. Each band shows the first three letters of the first entry on the page. Simply flick through the bands till you find the entry you need!

All the main entries are also cross-referenced to help you find them. Names in small capitals – **CHILDREN** – tell you that there is more information about the item you are looking for under the topic on children in the first part of the book. So when you read 'see **CHILDREN**' you turn to the blue heading for **CHILDREN**. The instruction 'see **A-Z**', after a word, lets you know that the word has its own entry in the second part of the book. Similarly words in bold type – **Alanya** – also let you know that there is an entry in the gazetteer for the indicated name. In both cases you just look under the appropriate heading in the red section. Packed full of information and easy to use – you'll always know where you are with your Collins Traveller Guide!

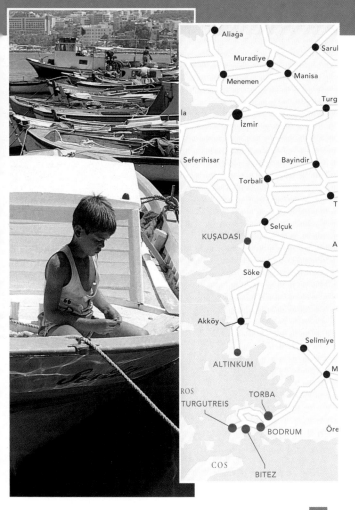

Aliaǧa

Sarul

Muradiye

Manisa

Menemen

Turg

İzmir

la

Seferihisar

Bayindir

Torbali

T

Selçuk

KUŞADASI

A

Söke

Akköy

Selimiye

ALTINKUM

M

ROS

TORBA

TURGUTREIS

BODRUM

Öre

COS

BITEZ

E ast is east, and west is west, and never the twain shall meet.' Thus goes the traditional saying, but in Turkey you will find that East and West do meet. Turkey, with a population of 54 million and an area of some 815,000 square km, occupies a unique position straddling the boundary between Europe and Asia. It is at once a bridge between East and West, and a colourful and distinctive culture in its own right. The country's history reaches back to the beginnings of civilization, but the Republic of Turkey that the traveller sees today dates from 1923, when the vision-ary leader Kemal Atatürk decided that his country's best chance of future stability and prosperity lay in modernization, pre-serving the best traditions of the imperial past, while looking increasingly towards the industrialized west as a model for development. His programmes of reform included the secularization of the govern-ment, the emancipation of women, and

the replacement of the Arabic script with a Latinized alphabet. His influence has been largely responsible for the country's present pros-perity compared with its Middle Eastern neighbours. Turkey is now a member of NATO, and has applied for membership of the European Community.

Turkey is rapidly increasing in popularity as a holiday destination. The growth in tourism over the past few years has been phenomenal: in 1988 over 4 million visitors arrived, nearly twice the number for 1986. In order to cope with this massive influx of holiday-makers, the devel-opment of resorts has been rapid and extensive; in almost every seaside town you will come across building sites as more and more villas and apartments go up. But fortunately the Turkish government has taken a far-sighted and responsible attitude towards development, realizing that the relatively unspoilt nature of the Turkish coast is one of its principal selling-points. Regulations forbid multi-storey hotels, and most new buildings complement rather than clash with their surroundings. As a result, in Turkey you will find few of the concrete eyesores that scar the waterfronts of the Costa del Sol and the Costa Brava.

Many companies offer competitively priced package holidays to the resorts on Turkey's Aegean and Mediterranean coasts. Some also offer 'two-centre' holidays, which provide the option of spending a week in Istanbul followed by a week at one of the seaside resorts. Travellers interested in sightseeing would do well to consider a 'fly-drive'

package; a car gives you the freedom to explore away from the beaten track, and is the ideal way to get the most out of a trip to this fascinating country. For those who want something a little different, there is the famous 'Blue Voyage': one or two weeks spent aboard a skippered Turkish yacht, cruising the stunningly beautiful coastline between Bodrum and Antalya. For the independent traveller too, Turkey makes an attractive destination. Getting around by public transport is easy and cheap, especially for students (who often qualify for discounts), food and accommodation are very cheap by European standards, and the people are friendly and welcoming.

What is it that is making Turkey so popular? The attractions are many. The climate on the coast is typically Mediterranean, with hot, sunny summers, and warm, clean waters that make the area a water sports

paradise. The beaches are always adequate, and often exceptional: who could resist the turquoise jewel of Ölü Deniz, or forget the vast, golden strand at Patara? The major resorts are sophisticated and cosmopolitan – in places like Bodrum and Marmaris you can rub shoulders with the jet set and dance the night away in Western-style nightclubs – and yet, only a few miles inland, you can find villages with a way of life that is totally Turkish, where the day begins at dawn with the muezzin's call to prayer. The cost of living is low compared with most other Mediterranean holiday areas, especially when it comes to eating out. Take advantage of this, because Turkish food is, quite simply, delicious. Forget the 'Turkish' kebabs you may have tasted back home; these insipid offerings cannot compare with the real thing, freshly grilled over charcoal and served with a rich tomato sauce, browned butter, yoghurt and a glass of *ayran*. And kebabs are only one delectable dish among many: Turkish cuisine is rated highly by gourmets.

The coastal scenery comes as a surprise to those who imagine Turkey to be a harsh and arid country. Between Kuşadası and Antalya the traveller can delight in varied vistas of spectacular mountain ranges rising to 2000-3000 m, often snow-capped until late in the summer; rocky hills clad in sweet-scented pine woods dropping steeply to the sea; and

fertile plains and river valleys planted with orchards, vineyards, figs, sunflowers, cotton, maize and tobacco. This rich and diverse landscape is steeped in a history that goes back nearly 10,000 years. The many civilizations and empires that rose and fell in this part of the world have left a rich legacy of impressive archaeological remains. Here you can explore the excavated streets of cities that feature in the writings of Herodotus and in the pages of the Bible, follow in the footsteps of Alexander the Great, and look out from castle battlements where the Knights of the Crusades once looked east towards the Holy Land.

The natural wonders are every bit as impressive as the man-made: the mile-long, sparkling-white, petrified cascades of Pamukkale's hot springs; the eternal flames of the Chimaera near Olympus, fed by natural gas from the bowels of the earth, and famed in Greek mythology as the fire-breathing monster slain by the hero Bellerophon; and the beautiful beach of Iztuzu, where loggerhead turtles lumber ashore each year to lay their eggs.

But Turkey's greatest asset is its people. The Turks are open, friendly, courteous and remarkably hospitable. They are proud of their country, and welcome visitors who take an interest in it. Although 99% of the population is Muslim, with an outlook on life very different from that in western Europe, the people are tolerant and understanding of western ways, and will go out of their way to make you feel comfortable. Most of the people you will meet in hotels, restaurants and the main resorts will be able to speak at least some English; in the countryside English speakers are fewer in number, but you can usually get by with smiles and sign language. The Turkish language is difficult to learn to speak fluently, but it is easy enough to get your tongue around the few simple words for 'hello', 'goodbye', 'please', 'thank you' and so on. It is well worth the effort – drop a few words of Turkish into your conversation and the Turks will love you for it!

Turkey is a large country – from Istanbul to the Mediterranean coast is around 1000 km – and in the space of two weeks the traveller can expect to see only a small part of it. But it is such a beautiful and enjoyable country that you will probably want to return again and again. Do so; after a few visits you will probably come to love the place as much as the Turks do themselves.

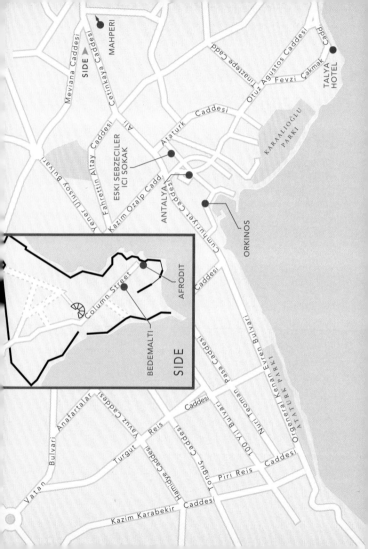

MAHPERI

TALYA HOTEL

Meviana Caddesi

SIDE

Çetinkaya Caddesi

Fahrettin Altay Caddesi

İnanözü Bulvarı

Yanel

Kazım Özalp Cadd.

ESKİ SEBZECİLER İÇİ SOKAK

Ali

Atatürk

ANTALYA Caddesi

Cumhuriyet Cadd.

Caddesi

Atatürk Caddesi

Otuz Agustos Caddesi

İnazıtepe Caddesi

Fevzi Çakmak Cadd.

KARAALİOĞLU PARKI

ORKINOS

AFRODIT

Column Street

BEDEMALTI

SIDE

Caddesi

Caddesi

Paşa Caddesi

Orgeneral Kenan Evren Bulvarı

ATATÜRK PARKI

Nuri Teoman

100 Yıl Bulvarı

İsabey Caddesi

Yavuz Caddesi

Anafartalar Caddesi

Turgut Reis Caddesi

Hamidiye Caddesi

Tonguç Caddesi

Piri Reis Caddesi

Vatan Bulvarı

Kazım Karabekir Caddesi

Restaurants

TALYA HOTEL Fevzi Çakmak Caddesi, Antalya.
❏ Expensive.
Antalya's top hotel offers luxury dining in a beautiful clifftop setting overlooking the sea.

ORKINOS Kale Ici Yat Limani (Old Harbour), Antalya.
❏ Moderate-expensive.
Enjoy a seafood dinner – sardines, octopus, or sokor, a delicious local fish, in the lovely atmosphere of the Old Harbour.

ANTALYA Behind Yivli Minare, off Cumhuriyet Caddesi, Antalya.
❏ Moderate.
Pleasant rooftop terrace near the 'Fluted Minaret', with view of the Old Town. Live Turkish music in the evenings.

ESKI SEBZECILER ICI SOKAK Antalya.
❏ Inexpensive.
You will find this narrow 'food street' in the Old Town is crammed with the tables of lively little restaurants selling basic but delicious Turkish food.

AFRODIT By harbour, turn right at foot of 'Column Street', Side.
❏ Moderate.
One of the best seafood restaurants in Side, with a nice terrace beside the sea. Swordfish is recommended.

BEDEMALTI 'Column Street', Side.
❏ Inexpensive.
The cheaper eating places are found away from the waterfront. Try Iskender Kebap: chunks of pide bread, doner and tomato with yoghurt and brown butter.

MAHPERI Gazi Paşa Caddesi, Alanya.
❏ Moderate.
Lovely setting on the promenade below the castle hill. Try out the local levrek (sea bass).

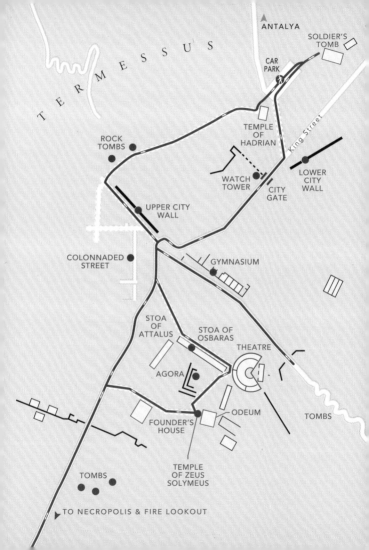

A 3-hr walk among the romantic, tumbled ruins of Termessus, the ancient mountain stronghold high in the hills above Antalya. Alexander the Great passed this way in 333 BC, took one look at its formidable defences, and went on his way without even attempting to take the city.

From Antalya, take the main road north to Burdur and Isparta, and after about 10 km turn left on the road to Korkuteli. In another 15 km you will reach the entrance to Termessos Milli Parki (Termessus National Park). From the gate, there is a steep drive uphill on an unsealed road for about 9 km to a parking area. The walk starts and finishes here. If you do not have private transport, you can take a bus from Antalya to the park entrance, from where it is a 2-hr walk to the upper parking area.

From the north end of the car park, a short path leads to the northern necropolis, where you will find the Soldier's Tomb, with beautiful carvings of lions. There are many other tombs scattered among the trees and bushes. Return to the car park, and take the left-hand of the two paths at the far end. This leads uphill to the lower city wall, and passes through the city gate, beside a fine watchtower. If you turn around and look up the hillside to the right, you will see the remains of an aqueduct that supplied the city with water. The path follows the line of the city's main road, called King Street. This leads to the upper city wall, a major structure to the right of the path. Climb up some steps beside the wall, and take the obvious path leading off to the left to look at the extensive remains of the gymnasium. If you follow this path for another five minutes, you come to the top of a zig-zag path which descends into the neighbouring valley, with many tombs scattered all around. Retrace your steps to King Street and turn left.

After a short distance, take the path forking uphill to the left, past a cistern, to reach the agora (marketplace). Near the path are the remains of the Stoa of Osbaras (a wealthy citizen of the city), and off to the right you will see the Stoa of Attalus (King of Pergamum). Near the latter are five deep cisterns used for water storage (approach these with caution, and keep young children well away from them). Continue along the path to the north of the agora and you will reach the top of the theatre, set in a magnificent position above a deep valley, and looking across to

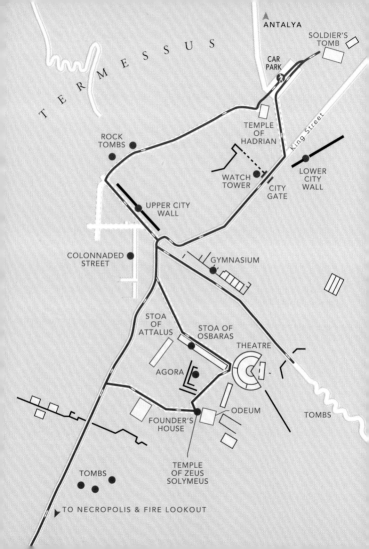

the twin peaks of Mount Solymus. This is a beautiful place to stop for a picnic lunch.

Pick your way across the agora, and through the rubble of earthquake-toppled buildings to look at the remains of the odeum (council chamber), Temple of Zeus Solymeus, and the Founder's House (an inscription on the doorway describes the owner as one of the city's founders). Trend back right towards the main path, and turn left, heading uphill. This path leads up through the upper necropolis, an awe-inspiring landscape of tumbled tombs, their lids awry, their walls smashed by grave-robbers, scattered about the hillsides like a scene from doomsday. The path continues all the way to a fire lookout hut at the top of the hill, from which you can enjoy glorious views to both north and south. Descend the path you came up, or alternatively detour to the right to explore more of the tombs before coming back down to the main path. Follow it down as far as the upper city wall, then turn left along the top of the wall, passing the overgrown remains of a colonnaded street on your left, before turning downhill at the foot of the cliff. This track takes you past several tombs carved into the rock face, before dropping down to the ruins of the Temple of Hadrian which are right beside the car park.

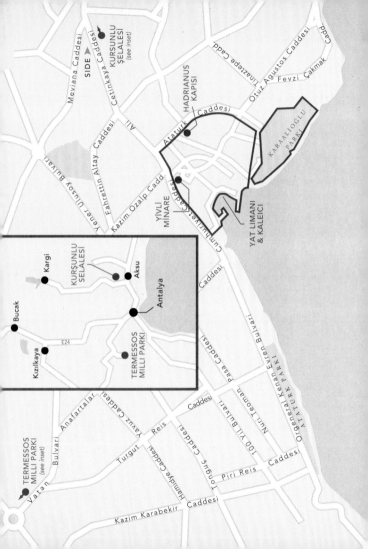

YAT LİMANI & KALEİCİ (OLD HARBOUR & OLD TOWN)
*The picturesque harbour, set into a recess in the cliffs below the walls of
the old citadel, and the maze of narrow streets rising behind it, have
been sympathetically restored by the Ministry of Culture and Tourism.
Dinner in one of the atmospheric restaurants at the harbour is a delight-
ful way to spend an evening.*

YİVLİ MİNARE Off Cumhuriyet Caddesi.
*The graceful 38 m-tall 'Fluted Minaret' is Antalya's best-known land-
mark. Built in 1230, its 8 columns of brown brick, decorated with pieces
of blue tile, rise above a 14thC mosque.*

HADRIANUS KAPISI (HADRIAN'S GATE) Atatürk Caddesi.
*This impressive marble gateway was built in AD 130 to commemorate
the visit of Emperor Hadrian. The gate is flanked by two massive towers,
part of the original 2ndC BC city wall.*

KARAALİOĞLU PARKI Otuz Ağustos Caddesi.
*This beautiful park is set on the clifftop above the harbour, with shady
promenades and masses of flowers, restaurants, tea gardens and a little
aviary. The view across the Gulf of Antalya to the Bey Dağları (the
mountains of the Olympus National Park) is beautiful, particularly at
sunset. At the western end is the Roman-built Hıdırlık Kulesi, a 17 m-tall
tower dating from the 2ndC AD, thought to be the remains of either a
lighthouse, or more probably the tomb of a local dignitary.*

KURSUNLU ŞELALESİ 20 km east of Antalya.
❑ 0800-1900. ❑ 400TL. Car.
*An attractive shady picnic area around a charming waterfall and old
mill; a good place for a cool, relaxing stroll. (But no swimming.)*

TERMESSOS MILLI PARKI
❑ 0800-1900. ❑ 10,000TL. Car or taxi.
*This park has a small museum, restaurant and camp site by the entrance,
and offers pleasant walking in the hills around the magnificent ruined
city of Termessus. See* ANTALYA-WALK, HISTORICAL SITES 2.

APHRODISIAS

A 1- or 2-hr walk around the beautiful remains of this ancient city, once dedicated to the worship of Aphrodite, goddess of love.

Aphrodisias (see **HISTORICAL SITES 1**) flourished from the 2ndC BC as a centre of the Aphrodite cult. Pilgrims would come from far and wide to take part in orgies to the goddess at the great Temple of Aphrodite. The cult eventually died out with the coming of Christianity, the temple was converted to a Christian basilica, and in the 6thC the city's name was changed to Stavropolis (City of the Cross). However, it was generally referred to as Caria, also the name of the surrounding region, which is echoed in the name of the neighbouring village, Geyre.

For details of how to reach the site, see **KUŞADASI-EXCURSION 2**. Excavation work is still in progress, and some parts of the site are closed to the public. Note that it is forbidden to take photographs of these active excavations. Begin by taking the path opposite the museum. This leads south past the recently excavated Sebasteion (a double portico dedicated to Aphrodite and the divine emperors of the Julio-Claudian family) and a colonnaded street, then climbs up the hill to the top of the well-preserved theatre. This hill is actually a man-made mound, and has been the site of a settlement for many thousands of years. Objects have been found here dating back as far as 5800 BC. From the top row of seats you can look down to the stage, paved in blue and white marble, with vaulted chambers behind (thought to have been dressing rooms). The chambers beneath the stage were used to keep wild animals for the brutal but popular shows of animal fighting. Beyond the stage, you can see a paved plaza surrounded by blue marble columns with a circular altar or fountain in the centre, which was probably used as a shopping mall and meeting place. To the south of the square are the Theatre Baths, and two lone columns further away mark the site of a gymnasium.

Follow the path round the top of the hill, from where you can look down onto the site of the agora (market and meeting place). Here graceful marble columns rise amid a stand of slender poplar trees, evoking an atmosphere of lost splendour. Looking north, beyond the Temple of Aphrodite you can see the stadium and the city walls in the distance. The path descends towards the massive masonry of the Baths

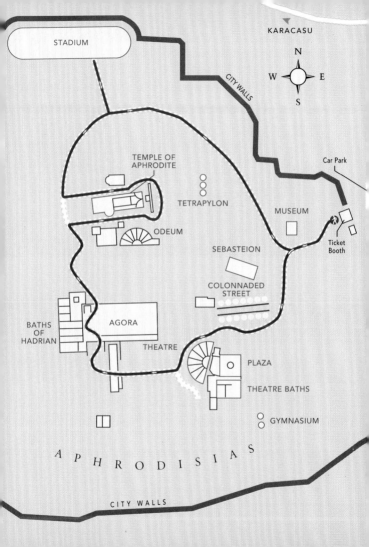

of Hadrian, winding through scattered blocks and broken marble columns. Inside you can explore the remains of marble-lined pools, bathtubs, chequered-tiled floors, and the under-floor heating system: hot air from fires flowed around the now-exposed piles of bricks that once supported the floors. From here, follow the track north, then detour to the right to look at the odeum, a mini-theatre used for concerts and plays, noting the lion's paws carved on the seats at the ends of the rows. Behind the odeum are the remains of the great Temple of Aphrodite, built during the 1stC BC and 1stC AD. Fourteen deeply fluted columns with Ionic capitals still stand, and two groups still support parts of the architrave. The structure around the well at the east end was added in the 5thC AD when the temple was converted to a Christian basilica.

Return to the main track and follow it round to the right until a path branching left across a field littered with fragments of broken columns leads to the stadium. This 30,000-seat structure is one of the best-preserved stadia in all of Asia Minor. It has 30 rows of seats, and measures 262 m long by 59 m wide. Go down into the middle and take a look at the sloping entrance tunnels at either end. Go back to the main track, which leads back to the museum and car park, passing the columns of the Tetrapylon, a ceremonial gateway on the approach to the Temple of Aphrodite.

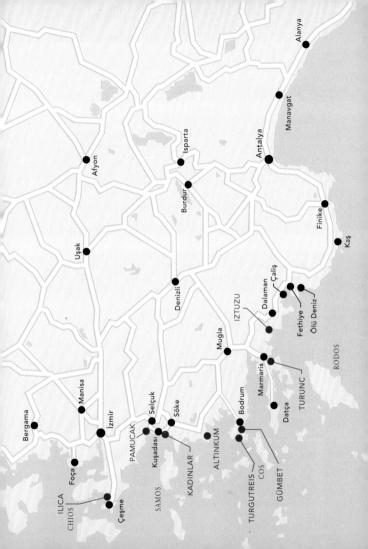

ILICA 5 km east of Çeşme. Dolmuş.
Several kilometres of soft, gently sloping sand backed by small resort town with cafés, bars, marina and thermal springs. Another good beach is at Altınkum/Tursite, 7 km south of Çeşme.

PAMUCAK 18 km north of Kuşadası. Car, irregular dolmuş.
Long, wide sweep of brown sand; little development as yet. Three motels nearby and a few food and drink stalls on the beach.

KADINLAR (LADIES' BEACH) 3 km south of Kuşadası. Dolmuş.
Long narrow strip of golden sand backed by bars, cafés, restaurants, hotels. Very popular. Umbrellas, sunbeds, and watersports facilities.

ALTINKUM 75 km south of Kuşadası. Dolmuş.
Beautiful, wide, sandy beach with excellent water sports facilities, seafood restaurants and bars. See **RESORTS-AEGEAN**.

GÜMBET 2 km west of Bodrum. Dolmuş.
Pleasant, tree-lined, coarse-sand beach set in calm, sheltered bay; safe for young children. Plenty of bars and restaurants, and several wind-surfing schools.

TURGUTREIS 20 km west of Bodrum. Dolmuş.
Lovely 1 km white-sand beach by small village with harbour, pensions, restaurants and a few shops. Good swimming, and beautiful views of Greek islands, especially at sunset. See **RESORTS-AEGEAN**.

TURUNÇ 10 km west of Marmaris. Dolmuş, boat.
Beautiful bay backed by a small village and steep mountains which offers a pleasant alternative to the more crowded beaches at Marmaris and neighbouring İçmele.

IZTUZU (DALYAN) 90 km southeast of Marmaris. Car.
One of the best beaches in the region, famous for the turtles which lay their eggs here in spring. 4 km of golden sand, and minimal facilities (toilets, drinks) at south end. See **MARMARIS-WHAT TO SEE**.

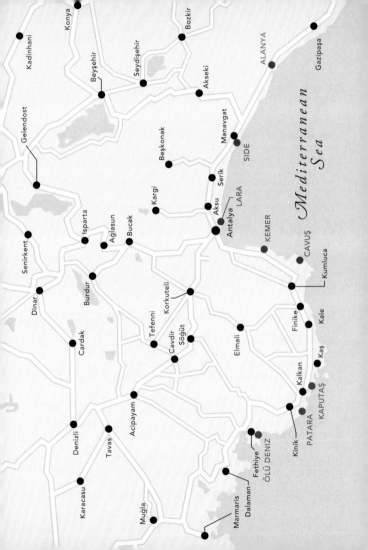

ÖLÜ DENIZ 12 km south of Fethiye. Dolmuş.
❑ 4000TL per car, 500TL per person.
White shingle beach on wooded spit between sea and lagoon.
Stunningly beautiful setting beneath steep hills. Very busy in summer.

PATARA 50 km northwest of Kaş. Dolmuş.
8 km of fine, white sand, backed by dunes and ruined city. No develop-
ment; facilities limited to two small restaurants, showers and toilets at
south end, and some umbrellas. See **A-Z.**

KAPUTAŞ 30 km west of Kaş. Dolmuş.
Lovely, tiny beach hemmed in by steep cliffs at mouth of spectacular
narrow gorge, reached by steps from main coast road. No facilities.

CAVUŞ 90 km south of Antalya. Car.
Secluded shingly beach in lovely bay below steep, pine-clad mountain,
with a few restaurants and pensions, and traditional boat-builders.

KEMER 50 km south of Antalya. Bus, dolmuş.
Long shingle beaches beside expanding modern resort town. Highly
developed, with vast range of facilities including sailing, windsurfing,
scuba-diving, water-skiing, etc.

LARA 12 km east of Antalya. Dolmuş.
Sandy bathing beaches with many motels, pensions, restaurants, bars,
etc. Gets very crowded at height of summer season.

SIDE 70 km east of Antalya. Bus, dolmuş.
Long, sandy beaches to east and west of town, good for families. West
beach has some shady trees, hotels, cafés, restaurants. East beach
stretches for several kilometres. See **RESORTS-MEDITERRANEAN.**

ALANYA 120 km southeast of Antalya. Bus, dolmuş.
Sweeping sandy beaches stretch east and west from the town, backed by
hotels, restaurants, bars, etc. Full facilities. West beach is cleaner and
has better swimming. See **A-Z.**

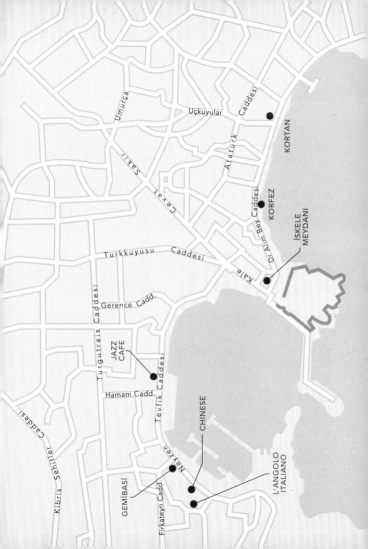

KORTAN Cumhuriyet Caddesi.
❏ Moderate-expensive.
This is a smart establishment offering excellent, if somewhat expensive, seafood dishes like swordfish kebab, octopus casserole and grilled prawns.

CHINESE Neyzen Tevfik Caddesi.
❏ Moderate-expensive.
You can't miss the bright red and white decor! Delicious Chinese dishes mean this place is often busy.

L'ANGOLO ITALIANO Neyzen Tevfik Caddesi, Yali Cikmazi.
❏ Moderate-expensive.
For those suffering pasta withdrawal symptoms, this quiet spot away from the crowded waterfront makes a pleasant change.

KORFEZ Dr Alim Bey Caddesi.
❏ Moderate.
Try the Bodrum speciality of trança şiş *(tuna kebabs) at this popular waterside restaurant.*

GEMİBASİ Neyzen Tevfik Caddesi.
❏ Moderate.
Typical waterfront restaurant serving seafood dishes. Pleasant pavement terrace opposite marina.

JAZZ CAFÉ Neyzen Tevfik Caddesi.
❏ Moderate.
More of a bar selling snacks, but a popular and lively spot, good for a few drinks and some light food.

İSKELE MEYDANI
❏ Inexpensive.
This is the main square below the castle, where you can find more than a dozen kebapcıs *and* pidecis *in the lanes leading away from the castle; good for cheap snacks like* şiş *kebap and* lahmacun *(Turkish 'pizza').*

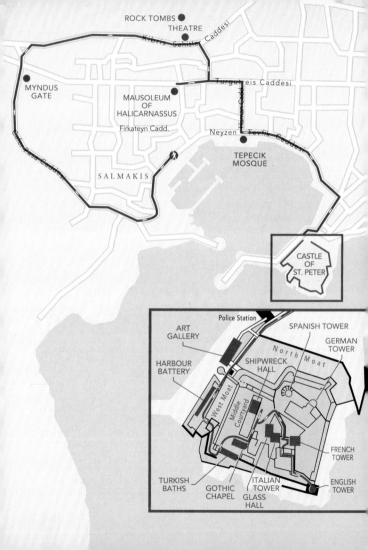

ROCK TOMBS

THEATRE

Kıbrıs Şehitler Caddesi

MYNDUS
GATE

Turgutreis Caddesi

MAUSOLEUM OF
HALICARNASSUS

Firkateyn Cadd.

Neyzen Tevfik Caddesi

TEPECIK
MOSQUE

SALMAKIS

CASTLE
OF
ST. PETER

Police Station

ART
GALLERY

SPANISH TOWER

GERMAN
TOWER

HARBOUR
BATTERY

SHIPWRECK
HALL

North Moat

West Moat

Middle
Courtyard

FRENCH
TOWER

ENGLISH
TOWER

TURKISH
BATHS

GOTHIC
CHAPEL

ITALIAN
TOWER

GLASS
HALL

A 2- to 3-hr walk around the historic sights of this attractive resort town.

Begin on the waterfront of the western bay opposite the marina. Follow the road away from town as it climbs and turns to the right into the suburb of Salmakis, then heads out of town (Cafer Paşa Caddesi). Nearby, now submerged in the western part of the bay, is the spring of Salamacis, whose waters were reputed to make men soft and effeminate. Legend has it that the son of Aphrodite, goddess of beauty, swam in a lake fed by the waters of the spring. Salamacis, the nymph of the lake, so fell in love with the youth that she begged the gods to allow her to live with him in a single body. Her wish was granted, and thus was created the half-male, half-female, Hermaphrodite.

Fifteen minutes' walk along Cafer Paşa Caddesi brings you to the ruins of the Myndus Gate. From here you can see the old city wall running up the hill in front of you. Continue to the main road and turn right to reach the restored theatre, which is still used today during festivals. From here you have a wonderful view over the twin bays of Bodrum and the imposing Crusader castle. Some of the seats have holes cut through them, probably for poles supporting sunshades. On the hillside above the theatre there are many rock tombs. Cross the main road and follow a narrow street opposite the theatre down to Turgutreis Caddesi and go right to visit the site of the Mausoleum of Halicarnassus (see **BODRUM-WHAT TO SEE**). Leaving the site, turn right, and then right again at Haman Caddesi, which leads to the waterfront at the pretty little Tepecik Mosque. Take a leisurely stroll along the quay to the left, and continue round to the entrance to the Castle of St. Peter (see **BODRUM-WHAT TO SEE**), built 1402-1513 by the Knights Hospitallers of St John of Jerusalem. It served as a mainland stronghold during the Crusades, second only to their principal stronghold on the island of Rhodes.

Enter via a ramp leading up behind the police station in the harbour square, passing the North Moat on the left and the art gallery on the right, to the ticket booth. Go through a passage and up another ramp to the right which leads to the top of the Harbour Battery. Notice that the walls around you contain many fragments salvaged from the ruins of the Mausoleum (greenish-coloured stone), and bear the arms of various

Grandmasters and Wardens of the castle. Cross the little bridge over the West Moat, and follow the path up and around to the left through the gate into the Middle Courtyard, past a souvenir stall. To the right is the Gothic chapel, completed in 1437. When the Ottomans took the castle in the 16thC a minaret was added and the chapel became a mosque. Today the building houses the Bronze Age Hall of the Museum of Underwater Archaeology (see **MUSEUMS**), with a display of objects recovered from the wrecks of two ships which sank in the 14th and

12thC BC. To the right of the chapel you will see a 19thC Turkish baths (*hamam*).

Go up the stairs to the left of the chapel and then up to the left, through an open-air display of amphorae. The building up to the right was once the Knights' dining hall and now contains a display of glassware dating from the 14thC BC-11thC AD. To the left is the Shipwreck Hall, housing the hull and cargo of an 11thC AD shipwreck found near Marmaris. Go through the gate in the wall beyond the Glass Hall and up the steps to the right to a door between two square towers. (Nearby are the Spanish Tower, also called the Snake Tower because it is decorated with carved serpents, and the German Tower.) On the right is the Italian Tower, which houses the Coin and Jewellery Hall, the Classical Period Hall and the Hellenistic Age Hall (including impressive bronze statues of a negro boy and of the goddess Isis, recovered from a wreck by sponge fishermen). On the left is the French Tower, containing the Yassi Ada Hall, which houses finds from two Byzantine shipwrecks of the 4th and

7thC AD. You can climb to the top of the French Tower for an excellent view over the castle and the town.

From the courtyard between the French and Italian Towers go up to the English Tower at the southeast corner of the castle, sometimes called the Lion Tower because of the lion carving on the west wall. Inside, the dimly-lit banqueting hall is hung with the banners of the Grandmasters and their Turkish enemies. The walk finishes here, where a 15thC atmosphere is evoked with incense, candlelight and medieval music.

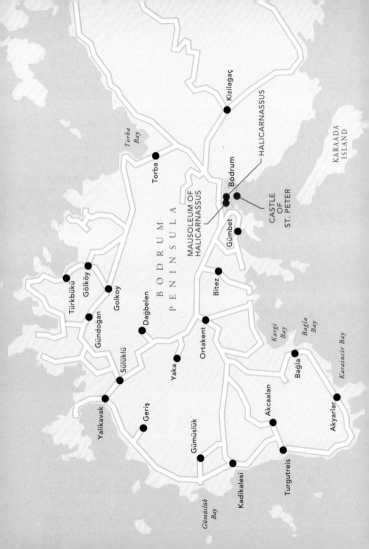

What to See

CASTLE OF ST. PETER

❏ 0800-1900. ❏ 5000TL.

Bodrum's Crusader castle, built in the early 15thC, dominates the harbour. Today, part of it houses the Museum of Underwater Archaeology, and a visit to the castle is a must. See BODRUM WALK, MUSEUMS.

HALICARNASSUS

Bodrum is built on the site of this ancient city, the birthplace of the historian Herodotus. Some ruins remain, notably the theatre, still in use today during festivals, the Myndus Gate, parts of the city wall, several rock tombs and the foundations of the Mausoleum. See BODRUM-WALK.

MAUSOLEUM OF HALICARNASSUS Turgutreis Caddesi.

❏ 0800-1200, 1500-1900. ❏ 1000TL.

Only the foundations remain of what was once one of the Seven Wonders of the Ancient World. Built for King Mausolus in the 4thC BC, it was destroyed, probably by an earthquake, some time in the 13th-14thC. The small museum at the site has a plaster model showing what the complete 55 m-tall structure must have looked like. See BODRUM-WALK.

BODRUM PENINSULA Accessible by car, dolmuş, boat.

The peninsula extending west of town is well worth exploring, with many pretty little villages and bays, and generally gravelly beaches. Clockwise from Bodrum are the popular beach resorts of Gümbet, Bitez and Ortakent, followed by the quieter bays of Kargı and Bağla, accessible by boat trips from town. The sandy beach and restaurants of Karaincir are close to the ruins of Cifik Castle, and the pretty fishing village and resort of Akyarlar. The town of Turgutreis has a good beach and several hotels, bars and restaurants, and nearby Gümüslük is surrounded by the scanty remains of ancient Myndus. The little restaurants by the bay are ideal for a sunset dinner. The road to Yalıkavak passes windmill-dotted hilltops before descending to the village, which is the biggest producer of sponges in Turkey, and has a 300-year-old windmill on the shore. The quieter villages of Gündoğan, Türkbükü and Gölköy have no beaches but there are some good fish restaurants, while Torba is a developing resort with a major holiday village.

*A 3- to 4-hr walk around the impressive remains of one of the most
important cities in the ancient world. See* **HISTORICAL SITES 1**, **Ephesus.**

Begin at the north entrance to the site (turn off the Selçuk-Kuşadası road
at the Tusan Efes Motel), where there is a large car park lined with souvenir shops, toilets, a restaurant, a post office and a currency exchange
booth. To the west of the car park, reached by a track near the toilets,
are the remains of the long narrow Church of the Councils. Originally
built in the 2ndC AD, probably as a museion (a centre for education
and research), a church was added at the west end in the 4thC AD, with
further additions and alterations in the 6th-7thC AD. This was the first
church to be dedicated to the Virgin Mary, and the Third Ecumenical
Council was held here in AD 431.

Enter the main site at the ticket booth and walk along the tree-lined
path that leads into the city. The open space on the right was occupied
by the largest building in Ephesus, the Halls of Verulanus, with a wide
courtyard where athletes once exercised. Beyond are the ruins of the
harbour gymnasium and baths, part of the same complex. But your eye
will be caught by the huge theatre rising to your left, beyond the broken columns of the theatre gymnasium. Before visiting the theatre, turn
right and take a stroll along the Arcadian Avenue, Ephesus' impressive,
600 m-long, colonnaded main street, constructed around AD 400. The
street had mosaic-tiled pavements down either side, and was lit at night
by oil lamps. Halfway down you will find the bases of four columns
which once bore statues of the four Evangelists. The site of the former
harbour, which silted up many centuries ago, is lost in the bushes at the
end of the street. Return along the avenue and explore the huge,
remarkably well-preserved 24,000-seat theatre, built during the 1st-
2ndC AD. This is probably where the riot of the silversmiths described
in Acts 19: 24-41 took place. The smiths reacted against the preachings
of St. Paul, because the spread of Christianity had resulted in the loss of
their trade in silver shrines for the goddess Diana (Artemis). Climb to
the top row of seats for a good view down the Arcadian Avenue to the
smooth plain that, 2000 years ago, was not land but sea. Below the
conical hill to the left is the site of the Bay of Ephesus, the harbour
which led to the city's great prosperity.

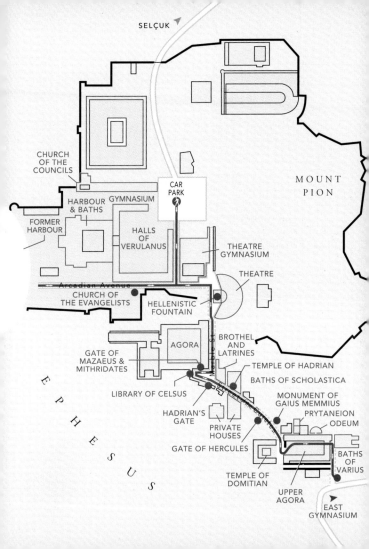

SELÇUK

MOUNT
PION

CHURCH
OF THE
COUNCILS

HARBOUR
& BATHS

GYMNASIUM

CAR
PARK

FORMER
HARBOUR

HALLS
OF
VERULANUS

THEATRE
GYMNASIUM

THEATRE

Arcadian Avenue

CHURCH OF
THE EVANGELISTS

HELLENISTIC
FOUNTAIN

BROTHEL
AND
LATRINES

AGORA

GATE OF
MAZAEUS &
MITHRIDATES

TEMPLE OF HADRIAN

BATHS OF SCHOLASTICA

LIBRARY OF CELSUS

MONUMENT OF
GAIUS MEMMIUS

E P H E S U S

HADRIAN'S
GATE

PRYTANEION
ODEUM

PRIVATE
HOUSES

GATE OF HERCULES

BATHS
OF
VARIUS

TEMPLE OF
DOMITIAN

UPPER
AGORA

EAST
GYMNASIUM

Outside the theatre is an attractive Hellenistic fountain (2ndC BC). Pass this and continue up Marble Street, paved over during the 5thC AD. Note the prominent ruts caused by the passage of countless wheeled carts; pedestrians used a raised colonnade on the right. At the end of this street, across the small square on the right, you come to the best-known building in Ephesus, the magnificently restored Library of Celsus. The library was built in the early 2ndC AD by a Roman Consul in memory of his father Gaius Julius Celsus Polemaeanus, whose body still lies in its tomb beneath the central niche in the rear wall. The 12,000 scrolls were stored in niches along the walls. To the left of the library is Hadrian's Gate, and to the right is the Gate of Mazaeus and Mithridates, the entrance to the agora (market square). This is a good spot to try to imagine what Ephesus might have been like in its heyday. Sit on the library steps and in your mind's eye people the streets with milling crowds, the clatter of cartwheels on the marble, and the shouts of vendors in the market.

Across the street from the square is a house that is
thought to have been a brothel – the figure of
Priapus on display in the Ephesus Museum in
Selçuk was found in the well in this house (see
MUSEUMS). There are some nice mosaic floors and
the remains of painted frescoes. Just uphill from this
house is a public latrines (currently being restored). Continuing up the
Street of the Curetes (temple priests), you pass a fountain and the octag-
onal tomb of a young woman on the right. On the left is the small but
pretty Temple of Hadrian, and the extensive Baths of Scholastica. The
right side of the street here has a beautiful, colonnaded, mosaic pavement in front of the remains of several small shops. Up the hill above
the shops are the ruins of a number of private houses that once
belonged to wealthy citizens. They contain some very interesting
mosaics and frescoes, but you must pay an extra admission fee to visit
them (0800-1600: 2000TL).
At the top of the Street of the Curetes is the Gate of Hercules, built in
the 4thC AD, and decorated with carvings of Hercules dressed in the
hide of the Nemean Lion. Go through the gate and head right, past the
Hydreion fountain and the Monument of Gaius Memmius to the
Temple of Domitian (1stC AD), which houses the Museum of
Inscriptions. Unfortunately, at the time of writing, the translations of the

inscriptions are given in Turkish and German only. Opposite the museum is the open square of the Upper Agora, lined on its north side by the Prytaneion (which housed the sacred flame of the city; the statues of Artemis displayed in the museum in Selçuk were found here), and the semicircular odeum, probably used for concerts and meetings of the city council. At the end of the colonnaded street running along the north side of the agora are the 2ndC AD Baths of Varius.

You could now retrace your steps to the car park, but a better way is to walk round the east side of Mount Pion. Exit the site at the south entrance, and head

left down the tarmac road past the bulky ruins of the East Gymnasium on the left, and the tumbled stones of the Magnesian Gate on the right. After about 300 m, turn left on a dirt road signposted 'Grotto of the Seven Sleepers'. This passes between fields and orchards, with a view across to the citadel of Ayasuluk above Selçuk town. When you reach the point where the road becomes surfaced (there is a cold-drinks stall here), follow a path up the hill to the left to reach the Grotto. Legend has it that around AD 250 seven young men of Ephesus took refuge in the cave to escape persecution of their Christian beliefs. They fell into a deep sleep and woke up 200 years later to find that Christianity had become the state religion. When they died they were buried in the cave, a church was built there, and the site became a place of pilgrimage. There are two levels: a lower vaulted chamber with many tombs; and what was probably the church above, where you can see a few remains of mosaic floor and plaster ceiling, and at the back some traces of red and blue fresco with painted writing. Return to the road and head left along the foot of the hill, turn left at the main road, and finish the walk back at the car park.

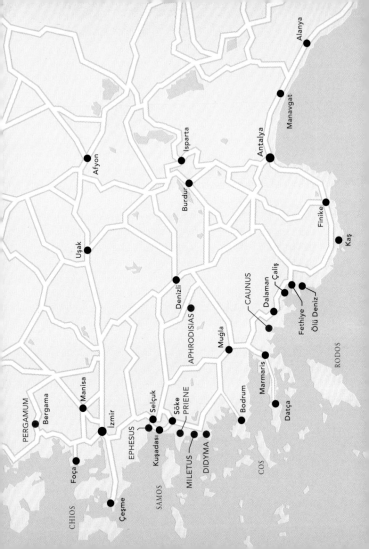

HISTORICAL SITES 1

PERGAMUM
❑ 0900-1730. ❑ 1000TL; Asclepieum 5000TL. Bus from İzmir.
Impressive remains of 2000-year-old hilltop city, extensively restored by German archaeologists. See KUŞADASI-EXCURSION 3, A-Z.

EPHESUS
❑ 0800-1700. ❑10,000TL. Dolmuş from Kuşadası.
Wander the streets of one of Turkey's most extensively excavated and restored ancient cities. See EPHESUS, KUŞADASI-WHAT TO SEE, A-Z.

PRIENE
❑ 0830-1930. ❑ 2000TL. Dolmuş from Kuşadası, via Söke.
Magnificent wooded setting on terrace below cliff, overlooking Plain of River Maeander. Lovely place for a stroll just before sunset. See A-Z.

MILETUS
❑ 0830-1930. ❑ 2000TL. Dolmuş from Kuşadası, via Söke.
Explore the large theatre, capped with the remains of a later Byzantine fortress, and the neighbouring caravanserai and well-preserved İlyas Bey Mosque, both dating from the 15thC. See A-Z.

DIDYMA
❑ 0830-1900. ❑ 2000TL. Dolmuş from Kuşadası, via Söke.
Remains of vast 2000-year-old Temple of Apollo, whose construction was ordered by Alexander the Great. See A–Z.

APHRODISIAS
❑ 0800-1730. ❑ 5000TL. Car or coach tour.
These ruins occupy a beautiful site on a high plain. Well-preserved theatre, baths, odeum and stadium. See APHRODISIAS, KUŞADASI-EXCURSION 2.

CAUNUS
❑ All times. ❑ Free. Boat from Köyceğiz or Dalyan.
Atmospheric former port now 5 km from sea, with impressive theatre and carved rock tombs. See MARMARIS-WHAT TO SEE.

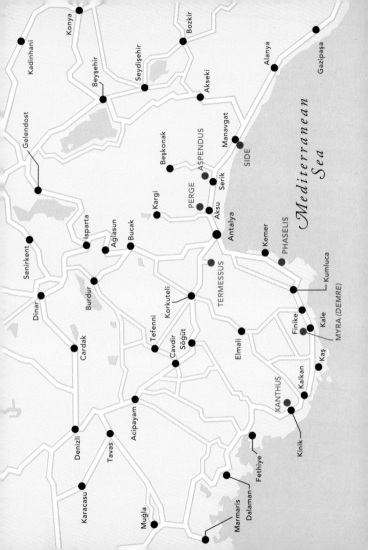

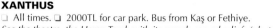

HISTORICAL SITES 2

XANTHUS
❑ All times. ❑ 2000TL for car park. Bus from Kaş or Fethiye.
See the theatre, the Harpy Tomb with its superb carved reliefs (plaster casts; originals in British Museum), and inscribed pillar tomb.

MYRA (DEMRE)
❑ All times. ❑ Free. Bus from Kaş.
Large, impressive theatre, and numerous richly decorated rock tombs carved into the cliff face beside it. See **Noel Baba Kilisesi.**

PHASELIS
❑ 0800-1730. ❑ 5000TL. Dolmuş from Kemer.
On a charming wooded site beside the sea. Ancient walls, streets, gateways, theatre and aqueduct rise among the trees and shrubs, making a picturesque picnic spot. Unfortunately very busy in high season.

TERMESSUS
❑ 0800-1900. ❑ 10,000TL. Car (bus from Antalya, then 2-hr walk).
Set in a wooded hollow 1000 m up in the mountains, the ruins of this ancient city are breathtaking. See **ANTALYA-WALK, WHAT TO SEE.**

PERGE
❑ 0900-1700. ❑ 5000TL. Car (bus from Antalya, then walk).
Enjoy the view of the city from the top of the theatre before going on to explore this fascinating site. See **A-Z.**

ASPENDUS
❑ 0800-1700. ❑ 5000TL. Car (bus from Antalya, then walk).
The magnificent 15,000-seat theatre is the best-preserved Roman theatre in existence. Events staged here during the Antalya Festival in May.

SIDE
❑ 0830-1700. ❑ 2000TL. Bus from Antalya.
One of the largest theatres in Anatolia, still in fairly good condition, and restored temples to Athena and Apollo add interest to this busy seaside resort. See **BEACHES 2, RESORTS-MEDITERRANEAN.**

*B a y
o f
İ z m i r*

ATATÜRK
MUSEUM

Talat Paşa Bulvarı

ST. JOHN'S
CATHEDRAL

Cumhuriyet Bulvarı

Şair Eşref Bulvarı

Cumhuriyet
Meydanı

ATATÜRK
STATUE

KULTURPARK

Şair Eşref Bulvarı

Dr. Refik Saydam Bul.

Gazi   Bulvarı

Mürşelpaşa Bul.

Basmane
Station

Fevipaşa   Bulvarı

Gaziler Caddesi

CITY
HALL

SADIRVAN
MOSQUE

Anafarta

SAAT
KULESI

Bulvarı

KONAK
CAMII

AGORA

KONAK
SQUARE

Cumhuriyet

Eşrefpaşa

ARCHAEOLOGICAL
MUSEUM

KADIFEKALE

*A one-day excursion from Kuşadası or Çeşme to İzmir (see **A-Z**), Turkey's third-largest city.*

Approaching from Kuşadası, leave the E 24 at the exit signposted Çeşme (opposite ruins of Sirinyer aqueduct), then follow signs for Konak. Eventually you will descend a swooping series of hairpin bends to the bustling Konak Square, passing near the foot of the hill the entrance to the Archaeological Museum. Arriving by bus, you will either go straight to Konak bus station, or to the *otogar* 4 km away, from where a shuttle service runs to Konak. You can visit the sights described here either on foot, by dolmuş, or by taxi.

Begin in Konak Square, the traditional city centre. At the north end, beside the ferry quay, is the 90-year-old Saat Kulesi (Konak Clock Tower), İzmir's symbol and best-known landmark, with the City Hall behind. Cross the pedestrian bridge and look at the pretty little Konak Camii (Konak Mosque), dating from 1754, before heading into the Kemeraltı (Old Bazaar) along Anafartalar Caddesi. This is one of Turkey's best bazaars; explore the side alleys if you have time, otherwise just follow your nose along Anafartalar Caddesi as it curves round to the left, taking in the colourful crowds, the smells of coffee, kebabs and cooking fish, the shops selling carpets, leather, shoes, clothes. If you turn right at Sadırvan Mosque you will exit onto the wide street of Esrefpaşa Caddesi. Turn right, then left on 816 Sokak which leads to the Agora, the marketplace of ancient Smyrna. The excavated remains here date from AD 178, when the town was rebuilt by Marcus Aurelius after an earthquake, and include 13 standing Corinthian columns and a three-aisled basilica. From the east end of the Agora, follow 941 Sokak to the continuation of Anafartalar Caddesi, and turn right, following this street round to the left past Basmane railway station and across the large roundabout to the Kültürpark (Culture Park). This huge park was built on the rubble of the old Greek quarter, destroyed in the fighting of 1922, and has many attractions, including shady walks, fountains, tea-rooms, restaurants, an amusement park and a small zoo. Each year in August-September it hosts İzmir's International Trade Fair. On Şehit Neveresbey Bulvarı, west of the park, is the Catholic St. John's Cathedral, built 1862-74, with a richly decorated interior. Continue

down this avenue to the waterfront at Cumhuriyet Meydanı (Republic Square), with its equestrian statue of Atatürk (see **A-Z**), and İzmir's top hotel, the Büyük Efes. From here you can stroll along Atatürk Caddesi, İzmir's stylish promenade, known locally as the Kordon, lined with modern shops and sophisticated restaurants. 800 m north of the square, past the South-Eastern Headquarters of NATO, is the Atatürk Museum, which contains an ethnographic display, and mementoes of the leader's stay in the city (Tue.-Sun. 0900-1200, 1300-1730: 400TL). Returning to Konak Square along the Kordon, walk up the hill opposite the bus station to visit İzmir's excellent new Archaeological Museum (see **MUSEUMS**), where you can admire sculpture and artefacts recovered from Smyrna, Ephesus, Pergamum, Miletus, etc. If time permits, take a dolmuş or taxi up to Kadifekale (Velvet Castle), old Smyrna's hilltop citadel. All that remain are the medieval walls, but the view over the city and the bay is breathtaking, especially as sunset approaches.

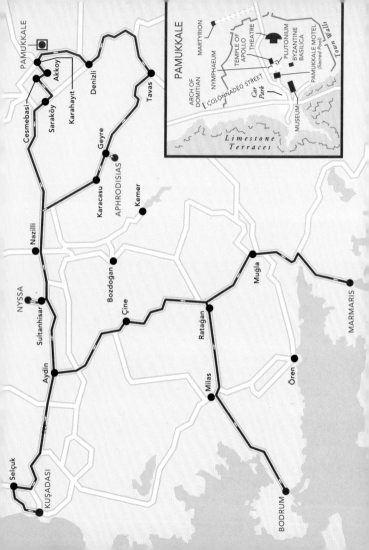

PAMUKKALE

MARTYRION
THEATRE
TEMPLE OF
APOLLO
PLUTONIUM
BYZANTINE
BASILICA
NYMPHAEUM
ARCH OF
DOMITIAN
COLONNADED STREET
Car
Park
Sacred Pool)
PAMUKKALE MOTEL
Town Walls
MUSEUM

Limestone
Terraces

PAMUKKALE
Çesmebasi
Akköy
Saraköy
Karahayit
Denizli
Tavas
Geyre
Karacasu
APHRODISIAS
Kemer
Nazilli
NYSSA
Bozdoğan
Muğla
MARMARIS
Sultanhisar
Çine
Ratağan
Aydin
Milas
Ören
Selçuk
KUŞADASI
BODRUM

A two- or three-day excursion from Kuşadası, Bodrum or Marmaris, visiting three ancient cities and a spectacular hot spring.

Head first towards the town of Aydın (65 km from Kuşadası, 166 km from Bodrum, 135 km from Marmaris), and drive east on the main E 24 road. Turn left at the village of Sultanhisar. (The following distances are measured from Aydın).

37 km – Nyssa. This ancient city was famous as a centre of education (0800-1730; 2000TL). Strabo (63 BC-AD 25), the Greek geographer and historian, studied grammar and rhetoric here. The approach road leads through the old city walls and the scattered tombs of the necropolis to a car park in front of the theatre. The setting is lovely: olive trees grow among the seats of the theatre, offering shade for a picnic lunch. It is a quiet spot away from the main tourist trail, the silence interrupted only by birdsong and the occasional barking dog in the village below. The view across the wooded remains of the city to the wide plain of the Büyük Menderes (River Maeander) is idyllic. On the far side of the car park are the ruins of the bouleuterion (council chamber), library, gymnasium and two Byzantine churches. A Roman tunnel leads under the road from the east end of the theatre. Return to the main road and continue east. Turn right 16 km beyond Nazilli, on road 585, through Karacasu, to the village of Geyre.

75 km – Aphrodisias. The little village of Geyre contains a few restaurant-pensions where you can stay the night after visiting the ruins of nearby Aphrodisias (0800-1730: ruins 5000TL, museum 5000TL). Chez Mestan, about 400 m before the turn-off to the ruins, is recommended. The owners speak fluent French and English. The excavations here have revealed extensive remains of the city, once dedicated to the worship of Aphrodite, goddess of love and beauty, and home to a famous school of sculpture, whose works have been found as far away as Rome and north Africa. See **APHRODISIAS**.

The road southeast from Geyre climbs into beautiful hill-country clothed in open pine-woods, then descends to a wide plain spiked with slender poplar trees. At Tavas, turn left and then left again at the main road, heading for Denizli. The final approach to the town descends a spectacular series of swooping hairpin bends with breathtaking views

of the surrounding mountains. At Denizli, follow signs for Pamukkale, which lies 18 km from the town.

180 km – Pamukkale. This series of glistening white calcareous terraces, deposited over the centuries by hot, mineralized springs, is one of Turkey's most famous and spectacular sights (car 2000TL). The name means 'Cotton Castle', a reference to the dazzling whiteness of the deposits (in Turkey, the expression 'as white as cotton' is equivalent to the English 'as white as snow'). The ruins of ancient Hierapolis, founded in the 2ndC BC by King Eumenes II of Pergamum, are scattered about the plateau above a petrified cascade of stalactites and warm pools. There is a large car park, many souvenir stalls, a few restaurants, and half a dozen motels which cater mostly to coach parties. The Pamukkale Motel is built around the so-called 'Sacred Pool', a bathing pool fed by hot springs (35°C), whose floor is littered with ancient marble columns. You can visit the pool even if you are not staying at the motel (1000TL). You can also bathe in the many shallow pools on the terraces, though the water leaves a deposit of glittering white powder on your skin and hair. The pools are very busy on weekends and public holidays. (NB You must remove your shoes before walking on the terraces, to help minimize erosion of the surface.) The waters are drinkable; they contain calcium, bicarbonate, sulphate and carbon dioxide, and are reputed to be good for disorders of the kidneys, heart and digestive system.

Beside the car park is the museum, housed in the restored Great Baths of Hierapolis (see **MUSEUMS**). The road that passes to the left of the Pamukkale Motel leads uphill towards the theatre. Just beyond the motel the road crosses the colonnaded main street of Hierapolis, leading to the Arch of Domitian away to the left. On the right are the remains of a nymphaeum (monumental fountain), and beyond it a Byzantine basilica. Above the nymphaeum is the ruin of the 3rdC AD Temple of Apollo, and next to the temple, on the side opposite the road, is the sinister Plutonium. A few steps lead down into a small square recess. At the back is a small doorway closed off by a metal grille, and a sign saying 'DANGER POISONOUS GAS'. From the slimy green chamber beyond the grille you can hear the hissing of a hidden stream which emits carbon dioxide vapours. In the days when Hierapolis flourished this was a sanctuary dedicated to Pluto, god of the underworld. The gas, being heavier than air, collected in the lower part of the chamber, and was capable of killing animals as big as cattle, and to this day dispatches any birds that stray inside. Uphill is the 2ndC AD theatre, and a few hundred metres further along the road is a track on the left leading to the Martyrion of the Apostle Philip, erected in the 5thC AD.

Leave Pamukkale by the road leading north to Karahayıt, through the extensive necropolis, littered with large and impressive tombs. At Karahayıt there are more hot springs (but no terraces), where the water is rich in iron, and stained red. Go left to Akköy, right to Çeşmebasi, then left again to reach the main road near Saraköy, from which you can return west to Aydın. Alternatively, if you want to spend the night at Pamukkale, go back down the hill to the village at the foot of the terraces where there are many pleasant and inexpensive pensions. (The motels at the top of the hill are usually booked solid with coach tours.)

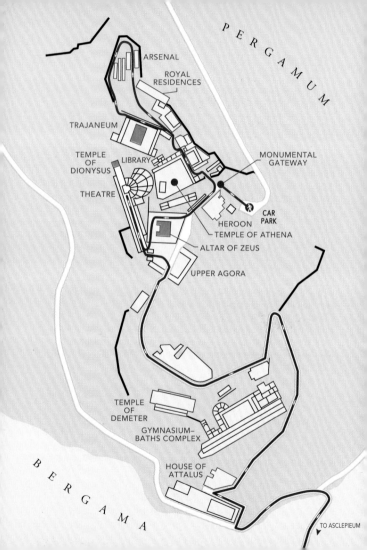

PERGAMUM

ARSENAL

ROYAL
RESIDENCES

TRAJANEUM

TEMPLE
OF
DIONYSUS

LIBRARY

THEATRE

MONUMENTAL
GATEWAY

CAR
PARK

HEROON

TEMPLE OF ATHENA

ALTAR OF ZEUS

UPPER AGORA

TEMPLE
OF
DEMETER

GYMNASIUM–
BATHS COMPLEX

HOUSE OF
ATTALUS

BERGAMA

TO ASCLEPIEUM

Excursion 3

*A one-day excursion from Kuşadası or Çeşme to the spectacular moun-
tain-top ruins of ancient Pergamum (see **HISTORICAL SITES 1**, **A-Z**).*

From Kuşadası follow the E 24 main road north through İzmir for
180 km, then turn right on road 240 to the modern market town of
Bergama. On the outskirts of town, on the left of the main street at the
point where it becomes a dual carriageway, is the Tourist Information
Office. About 600 m further on is the Bergama Museum, which has a
fine collection of sculpture and artefacts recovered from excavations at
Pergamum (0900-1730; 2000TL). Follow the main street through the
town centre, where it becomes very narrow and twisting, across the
river, and up the steep hill to the acropolis (0900-1730; 1000TL), the
site of the old Greek city. Excavation and restoration of the site by
German archaeologists began in the late 19thC and continues today;
much material has been removed to the Pergamon Museum in East
Berlin.

From the car park (souvenir stalls, cold drinks, postcards, guidebooks,
etc.), a ramp leads up past the Heroon, where the kings of Pergamum
were honoured, to the remains of a monumental gateway, and into the
main part of the city. There are helpful notice-boards dotted around the
site, with maps and historical information. Down on the left is a wide
open space littered with column stumps, the site of the 4thC BC Temple
of Athena, and beyond it (fenced off and undergoing restoration) the
famous Library, which is thought to have held 200,000 volumes. It was
subsequently presented by Anthony to Cleopatra, adding to the wealth
of the Library of Alexandria. On the right of the path are the remains of
five royal residences, each consisting of rooms arranged around a
colonnaded court. Look out for the deep cisterns used for water storage. Beyond the houses, at the highest point of the hill, is the Arsenal,
where you can see the outlines of the narrow storage rooms. From the
city walls here, you can enjoy a magnificent view across the valley of
the Caicus river, and trace the remains of the remarkable aqueduct system that carried water to the city from the mountains of Madra Dağ,
over 45 km to the north.

Retrace your steps to the Trajaneum, Pergamum's most impressive
building, recently restored. Built on a large terrace supported by huge

vaults (which can be visited via steps below the terrace), the temple was dedicated to the Emperors Trajan (AD 98-117) and Hadrian (AD 117-138). There are good views from the terrace over the theatre to the town of Bergama. Return to the monumental gateway, and go right down a path that leads to the site of the Altar of Zeus. Only the stepped foundation remains, shaded by a few pine trees, the rest having been removed to Berlin. The path continues past the upper agora, down to the promenade street which leads past the striking theatre, whose 80 rows of seats are set into the steep hillside. In the street below you can find the holes that once held the wooden posts supporting the removable stage. At the far end of the street are the ruins of a temple to Dionysus. From the upper agora, the path leads down to the lower part of the city, where you can explore the ruins of a gymnasium-baths complex, the Temple of Demeter and the House of Attalus (if you have your own car, you can drive down and park nearby, rather than climb back up to the upper car park).

On the way back through town, stop to visit the Kızıl Avlu (Red Hall). This massive red-brick structure dates from the reign of Hadrian in the 2ndC AD, and is thought to have been a temple dedicated to the Egyptian god Serapis. A double tunnel carries the river underneath the

ASCLEPIEUM

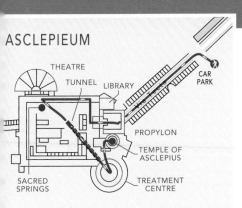

complex, which consists of a large courtyard (partly covered by present-day houses) and the huge basilica, whose walls stand almost 20 m high. Inside the basilica are the ruins of a later, smaller church dedicated to St. John the Apostle. After a visit to the museum, take the road that heads uphill beside the Tourist Office. This leads in 2 km to the remains of the Asclepieum (0900-1730: 5000TL). This was a great spa and medical centre that flourished in Roman times, when the great physician Galen (AD 129-200) practised here. The sick would come here and sleep in the temple, when Asclepius, god of healing, would appear in their dreams. The dreams were interpreted by priests and doctors, who then prescribed treatments which included drinking and bathing in the spring waters, mud-baths and herbal preparations. From the car park you walk along the paved, colonnaded Via Tecta, or Sacred Way, to the propylon, or entrance gate, where steps lead down into the courtyard of the Asclepieum. On the right, fenced off, are the ruins of the library, and from there the north gallery, lined with columns, leads to the 3000-seat theatre. In front of the theatre are the sacred springs, where you can still drink today. Enter the tunnel near the springs, and follow its eerie passage, lit by shafts of sunlight shining through holes in the roof, to a large circular building thought to be where medical treatments were carried out. You can see six semicircular niches where statues once sat, and stone tubs for bathing. Next door is the circular Temple of Asclepius, which had a 24 m-wide domed roof, where patients gave thanks to the god before leaving the Asclepieum.

GÜVERCIN ADA
(PIGEON ISLAND)

PIGEON ISLAND
RESTAURANT

*Kuşadası
Bay*

KISMET
HOTEL

Güvercin Ada Cadd.

ÖZ URFA
KEBAPCI

Atatürk Bulvarı

Kubris

CAM

Barbaros H. Cadd.

CLUB
KERVANSARAY

50- Yil Sokaği

Asanlar

Saalik

OSCAR
OCAMBASI

İnönü

CATI

Yildirim

Yeni Aydin

Kahramanlar

Çevre Yolu

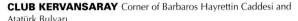

Restaurants

CLUB KERVANSARAY
Corner of Barbaros Hayrettin Caddesi and Atatürk Bulvarı.
❑ Expensive.
Dine in style in the courtyard of this 17thC Ottoman caravanserai. Live cabaret show every night.

KISMET HOTEL
Islet Mecilik ve Ticaret, 3 km east of town centre.
❑ Expensive.
Luxury establishment with palm trees and gardens overlooking harbour and marina; open to non-residents.

OSCAR OCAMBASI
Saalik Caddesi.
❑ Moderate.
Bright, bustling and popular, with tables on pavement, and on two floors inside. White-shirted waiters in black waistcoats dish up delicious traditional Turkish food.

CAM
Seafront, opposite end of Barbaros Hayrettin Caddesi.
❑ Moderate.
Pleasant and friendly, in nice setting overlooking the harbour. If too crowded, try neighbouring Toros and Diba restaurants, offering similar fare of meat and seafood dishes.

ÇATİ
Barbaros Hayrettin Caddesi.
❑ Moderate.
Rooftop restaurant with good views over town and harbour.

PIGEON ISLAND RESTAURANT
Güvercin Ada.
❑ Moderate.
Pleasant setting, with outdoor tables looking across bay to town. Try the mouthwatering kılıç şiş (swordfish kebabs).

ÖZ URFA KEBAPCI
Cephane Sokak.
❑ Inexpensive.
Good, cheap place offering usual range of kebabs, vegetable dishes, yoghurt, etc.

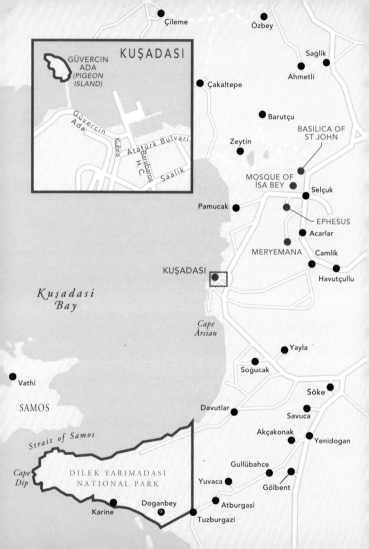

What to See

GÜVERCIN ADA (PIGEON ISLAND) Along causeway from
Güvercin Ada Caddesi.
*This scenic little island has the remains of a Byzantine fortress, a
lighthouse, a couple of restaurants and bars, and a disco. It is a popular
spot for an evening stroll.*

EPHESUS 16 km northeast.
❑ 0800-1700. ❑ 10,000TL. Dolmuş.
*Magnificent ruins of what was once the wealthiest city in Asia, dedicat-
ed to the worship of the goddess Artemis. Beside the road on the outskirts of Selçuk are the disappointing remains of the Artemision, the
great Temple to Artemis that was once one of the Seven Wonders of the
Ancient World. See EPHESUS, HISTORICAL SITES 1, A-Z.*

BASILICA OF ST. JOHN Selçuk. 20 km northeast.
❑ 0830-1700. ❑ 5000TL. Dolmuş.
*On the hill of Ayasuluk above Selçuk are the remains of a 6thC basilica
containing the tomb of St. John the Theologian who died at Ephesus
c. AD100. Above the basilica are the ramparts of a Byzantine citadel,
offering good views over town and plain.*

MOSQUE OF İSA BEY Selçuk. 20 km northeast.
*Below Ayasuluk is this huge, restored mosque, dating from 1375, with
unusual architecture, including granite columns taken from the harbour
baths at Ephesus.*

MERYEMANA 28 km east.
❑ 0800-1700. ❑ 1000TL, plus 400TL for car park.
*This place of pilgrimage is believed to be the house where the Virgin
Mary spent the last years before her death. Beautiful setting among trees
on hilltop. There is a small restaurant and post office.*

DİLEK YARIMADASI NATIONAL PARK 30 km south. Car.
❑ 0800-1800. ❑ 4000TL.
*Beautiful wooded peninsula fringed by lovely sand and shingle beaches
with parking and picnic areas, toilets and showers. Good swimming.*

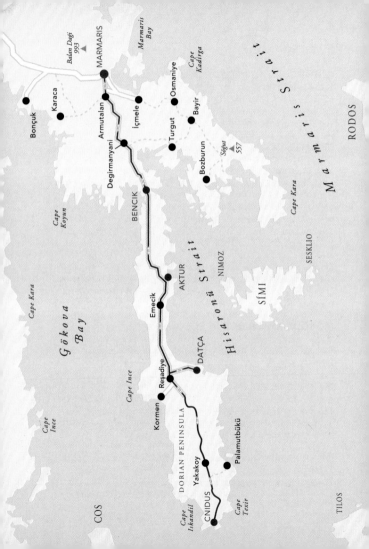

A one-day excursion from Marmaris, exploring the Dorian Peninsula (see MARMARIS-WHAT TO SEE), the spectacular finger of land that separates the Aegean and the Mediterranean.

There is a regular bus service between Marmaris and Datça, and there are daily boat trips from Marmaris to Datça and Cnidus. There is also a ferry service from Bodrum to Körmen Limanı, with a connecting bus to Datça, and regular boat trips from Datça to Cnidus. If using private transport, note that the unsurfaced road from Datça to Cnidus is very rough, and suitable only for 4WD vehicles, although the Datça taxi drivers may take you there for around 50,000TL round trip.

Take the road west from Marmaris (signposted 'Datça'). Soon the sea comes into sight as you approach the little hamlet of Bencik. Here the peninsula is only about 800 m wide, and in the 6thC BC the people of Cnidus tried to cut a channel across this neck of land as a defence against the invading Persians. The drive from here on is breathtaking, and requires a cool head and a steady hand: a narrow, twisting road climbs to the crest of the mountainous peninsula, with sweeping views of hills and sea, skirting steep crags of rust-brown rock, and winding through shady pine-woods with clearings where you will see the bee-hives that produce Marmaris's famous *çam balı* (pine-scented honey).

50 km – Aktur. As the road swoops down to the sea, you will see a lovely sandy beach backed by a wooded camp site (Aktur Mocamp). This is a lovely place to stay for those equipped with camping gear. The road continues, just as spectacularly, as far as Reşadiye, where you turn left to reach Datça.

70 km – Datça. This pretty little village is an increasingly popular holi-day resort, and offers a more peaceful alternative to bustling Marmaris. There are a couple of hotels, a holiday village (Club Datça), dozens of pensions and several good restaurants. The Tourist Information Office on the main square has details of accommodation, but note that the vil-lage is often full in summer. There is a pleasant harbour, with a pebbly beach, but not much to see. Datça is essentially a place to eat, drink and relax. To continue to Cnidus, return to Reşadiye and turn left. The road deteriorates rapidly as it enters the mountainous western part of the Dorian Peninsula, where strange-shaped limestone peaks rear up all around. The road passes through a couple of remote villages and many groves of olive trees, and there are a number of side roads leading to quiet bays with sandy beaches and little restaurants (e.g. Palamutbükü). At last, after a long and tiring drive, you arrive at Cnidus.

110 km – Cnidus. At the road end you will find a public telephone, a police hut, four restaurants, a pension, a couple of shacks and the scattered ruins of the ancient settlement of Cnidus. The city was originally situated near present-day Datça, but around 360 BC the inhabitants moved to this site at the very tip of the Dorian Peninsula. The move was made for sound commercial reasons, as northbound sailing ships could not round the cape against the prevailing northwest winds, and often had to wait for several days in Cnidus's south harbour. This snug bay is separated from a similar bay just to the north by a narrow isthmus which connects the mainland to a little island capped by a modern lighthouse. The northern bay is the so-called Trireme Harbour, which is thought to have held the ships of the Cnidian navy. Cnidus was a noted centre of scientific learning, and was home to the philosopher, astronomer and mathematician Eudoxus, and to Sosistratus, who designed and built the Pharos lighthouse at Alexandria, one of the Seven Wonders of the Ancient World. On the island are the remains of private houses, and there is an impressive Roman tomb near the lighthouse. On the mainland there are the remains of the city walls, the theatre and odeum, and other buildings, though little is left standing. About 200 m north of the Trireme Harbour, near where the city wall comes down to the sea, is the base of the circular 4thC BC Temple of Aphrodite, goddess of love and beauty. This temple once housed the famous nude statue of Aphrodite by the Athenian sculptor Praxiteles. Said to have been modelled on the sculptor's mistress, the statue was so beautiful that it became one of the world's earliest tourist attractions, and people travelled from far afield just to see it. Unfortunately, the statue has never been found, though archaeologists have discovered pieces of the plinth on which it stood. After exploring the ruins, take a swim from the jetty in the south harbour and enjoy a seafood dinner in one of the little restaurants before making the long drive back to Marmaris.

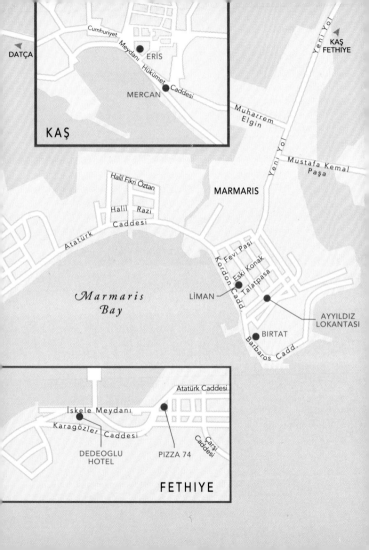

BIRTAT Barbaros Caddesi, Yat Limanı (Yacht Harbour), Marmaris.
❏ Moderate-expensive.
One of the best restaurants in town, with its large shaded terrace beside the moored yachts in the harbour. The seafood is delicious, as are the Turkish specialities.

LİMAN Kordon Caddesi, Marmaris.
❏ Moderate.
No outside tables, but the selection of basic Turkish dishes is delicious and reasonably priced.

AYYILDIZ LOKANTASI Haci Sabri Sokak, Marmaris.
❏ Inexpensive.
A good, cheap kebab restaurant in the bazaar area opposite the Tourist Information Office.

DEDEOGLU HOTEL İskele Meydanı, Fethiye.
❏ Moderate.
Rooftop restaurant overlooking the picturesque harbour, serving the usual range of Turkish dishes.

PIZZA 74 Atatürk Caddesi, Fethiye.
❏ Inexpensive-moderate.
Lively and popular place with pavement tables, serving traditional local fare as well as pizzas.

MERCAN Cumhuriyet Meydanı, Kaş.
❏ Moderate.
Popular seafood restaurant in good position beside the harbour. Sample the eponymous mercan, a delicious local fish.

ERİS Cumhuriyet Meydanı, Kaş.
❏ Inexpensive-moderate.
There is a nice atmosphere at this restaurant, with its tables on a leafy terrace looking across the square to the harbour. Try out the balık köfte *(grilled fish-balls).*

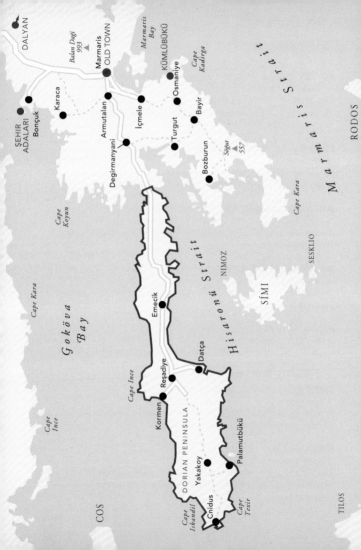

What to See

OLD TOWN

*The picturesque white houses and narrow streets of the Old Town hud-
dle around a small medieval fortress, built by Suleyman the Magnificent
in 1522. The streets have a bazaar-like atmosphere, crammed with little
shops and cafés, while more expensive restaurants and hotels line the
waterfront of the large yacht harbour.*

KÜMLÜBÜKÜ 10 km south of Marmaris. Boat.

*This peaceful, scenic bay is a popular stopping place on boat trips from
Marmaris. There are a few small hotels, restaurants and bars, and on a
nearby headland you can explore the ruins of ancient Amos, including
the city wall with gate and tower, a small temple and the theatre.
Nearby is another small bay, known as the Akvaryum (Aquarium)
because of its crystal-clear waters, a great place to stop for a swim.*

DORIAN PENINSULA West of Marmaris. Car or dolmuş.

*This finger of land projecting westward from Marmaris offers a spectac-
ular day trip by road or by boat. The main attractions are the pretty resort
village of Datça, and the ruined city of Cnidus at the very tip of the
peninsula. There are a number of beaches, perhaps the best being that at
Aktur. See* **MARMARIS-EXCURSION.**

ŞEHIR ADALARI 20 km north of town. Car to Taş Bükü, then boat.

*These 'Islands of the City' are so named because the largest of them
holds the remains of ancient Cedreae. The ruins include walls and
watchtowers, theatre and temple, in a romantic setting on the tiny, tree-
covered island. In the bay on the north side of the island is Cleopatra's
Beach. Legend has it that the sand on this beach was brought by the gal-
ley-load from Egypt at the order of Mark Anthony, to create a more
beautiful beach for his lover.*

DALYAN 90 km southeast by car, 40 km by boat.

*A popular boat trip goes up the scenic Dalyan river, visiting the rock
tombs and ruins of ancient Caunus (see* **HISTORICAL SITES 1**), *on into Lake
Köyceğiz for a swim, then back to Iztuzu beach, one of the last breeding
grounds of the Mediterranean loggerhead turtle. See* **BEACHES 1**.

Alanya

SIDE
MUSEUM

Manavgat

Isparta

Afyon

Antalya

Burdur

ANTALYA
MUSEUM

Finike

Kaş

Uşak

HIERAPOLIS
MUSEUM

Denizli

Çalış

Dalaman

Muğla

Fethiye

Ölü Deniz

RODOS

ARCHAEOLOGICAL
MUSEUM

EPHESUS
MUSEUM

Marmaris

Bergama

Manisa

Selçuk

Söke

Bodrum

Datça

İzmir

Kuşadası

COS

Foça

MUSEUM OF
UNDERWATER
ARCHAEOLOGY

SAMOS

CHIOS

Çeşme

ARCHAEOLOGICAL MUSEUM Paşa Caddesi, near Konak Square, İzmir.
❏ 0900-1730. ❏ 2000TL.
Pleasant, modern and well laid out, exhibits are labelled in Turkish and English. Sculpture and pottery ranges from prehistoric to Byzantine, with many finds from ancient Smyrna, Pergamum and Ephesus. See KUŞADASI-EXCURSION 1.

EPHESUS MUSEUM Selçuk.
❏ 0830-1830. ❏ 5000TL.
Excellent exhibits of finds from ancient Ephesus, with informative labels in English. Atmospheric hall displays sculpture relating to the goddess Artemis. Visit here before going to Ephesus itself. See EPHESUS.

MUSEUM OF UNDERWATER ARCHAEOLOGY Castle of St. Peter, Bodrum.
❏ 0830-1200, 1500-1900. ❏ 5000TL.
Nicely displayed collection of objects recovered from submarine excavations, including ancient cargos and reconstructed ships. See BODRUM-WALK.

HIERAPOLIS MUSEUM Pamukkale.
❏ 0900-1200, 1330-1700. ❏ 5000TL.
Housed in the impressive vaulted rooms of the Great Baths of ancient Hierapolis, it contains statuary, sarcophagi, jewellery and coins recovered from surrounding excavations. See KUŞADASI-EXCURSION 2.

ANTALYA MUSEUM Kenan Evren Bulvarı, Antalya.
❏ Tue.-Sun. 0830-1200, 1330-1700. ❏ 5000TL.
Collection of archaeological and ethnographic exhibits, including statuary from Perge and relics of St. Nicholas. See **Noel Baba Kilisesi**.

SIDE MUSEUM Side.
❏ 0830-1145, 1300-1700. ❏ 5000TL.
Housed in restored 5thC AD Roman baths. Beautifully displayed sculpture and sarcophagi, with lovely, shady garden at the back.

OLYMPUS

A 1- or 2-hr walk around the riverside ruins of the city of Olympus, followed by a 3-hr round trip to the eternal fire of the ancients.

Olympus is about 80 km south of Antalya, and about 120 km east of Kaş. Begin at the village of Çıralı, reached by an unsealed road (passable to most vehicles) which leads past the Chimaera Motel to a scattering of little pensions and snack bars at the beach (after crossing the bridge at the foot of the valley, turn right to park). Alternatively, take the road to Cavuş (about 100 m south of the fork to Çıralı), and after 8 km fork left (signposted 'Olympos') on an unsealed road (4WD recommended; avoid early in year as there are fords to cross, though the river dries up in summer) which leads through a lovely wooded valley to a parking area about 150 m from the sea. Those without private transport can take a bus to the Çıralı turn-off, from where it is a 90-min walk to the beach at Çıralı.

From Çıralı, go onto the shingle beach and head along to the right. After about 250 m you will reach the mouth of a valley, with a pierced rock in the cliffs at its right side, and a lagoon behind a shingle bar. This is the site of ancient Olympus (one of many ancient cities to take this name), which prospered between the 1stC BC and 2ndC AD. On the clifftop above the pierced rock you can see the walls of the acropolis. Most of the ruins are overgrown with thickets of laurel, fig and oleander, but this only adds to the romantic atmosphere of this beautiful spot. On the south side of the lagoon, find a faint track leading into the bushes, and follow it as best you can along the river bank. You will pass the remains of a warehouse, a Byzantine church and the theatre. In the stream opposite the church is a ruined bridge which once connected the two parts of the city. Follow the river bed upstream to a parking place (approachable from the Cavuş road, see above). From here a good path leads along the north bank of the river back to the beach. To the north of the path are the ruins of a gymnasium-baths complex with some interesting mosaics, and an impressive temple gate. Return along to the beach to Çıralı.

The next part of the walk, to the eternal flames of the Chimaera (*Yanartaş*, or burning rock, in Turkish) involves some uphill walking on a rocky path, and needs good walking shoes or boots. Return to the

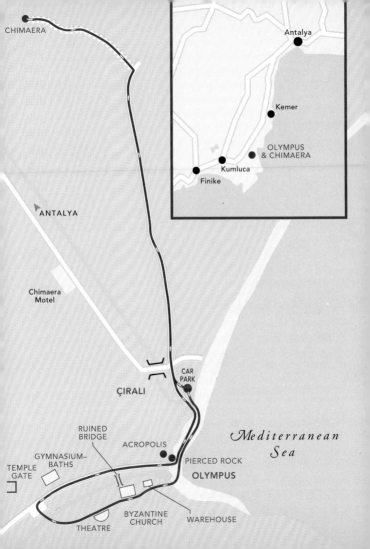

CHIMAERA

ANTALYA

Chimaera
Motel

CAR
PARK

ÇIRALI

RUINED
BRIDGE

ACROPOLIS

GYMNASIUM–
BATHS

PIERCED ROCK

TEMPLE
GATE

OLYMPUS

THEATRE

BYZANTINE
CHURCH

WAREHOUSE

Mediterranean
Sea

Antalya

Kemer

OLYMPUS
& CHIMAERA

Kumluca

Finike

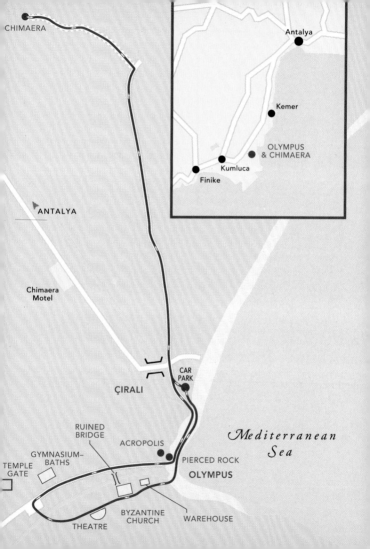

CHIMAERA

Antalya

Kemer

OLYMPUS
& CHIMAERA

Kumluca

Finike

ANTALYA

Chimaera
Motel

CAR
PARK

ÇIRALI

Mediterranean
Sea

RUINED
BRIDGE

ACROPOLIS

GYMNASIUM–
BATHS

PIERCED ROCK

TEMPLE
GATE

OLYMPUS

BYZANTINE
CHURCH

WAREHOUSE

THEATRE

bridge, and go straight past without crossing it. Keep left, on a dirt road that follows the foot of the hill, with a flat plain on the right, for about 2 km. Turn left just beyond the last house on the left and follow a rough track towards the woods (4WD vehicles can drive this far). Follow a path leading into the woods (waymarked with red dots), which begins to climb up the hillside to the left. A climb of about 30-40 min leads to

a clearing about 50 m wide, where you will find several small holes, less than a metre across, in which the perpetual flames burn. They are a freak of nature, fed by natural gas seeping through a fault in the rock, but in ancient times when the gas pressure was greater and they burned more fiercely, they were associated with the legend of the Chimaera, a fire-breathing beast, part lion, part goat, part snake, that was slain by the hero Bellerophon on his winged steed Pegasus. Nearby are the ruins of a Byzantine basilica, and an older temple to Hephaestus, the god of fire and the blacksmith's forge. Return down the same path to Çıralı.

CHIOS

Karaburun

Foça

Aliağa

Muradiye

Saruhanli

Menemen

Manisa

Urla

İzmir

Turgutlu

Salihli

ÇEŞME

Seferihisar

Bayindir

Ödemis

*Aegean
Sea*

Torbali

Tire

SAMOS

Selçuk

Aydın

KUŞADASI

Söke

FOÚRNOI

PATMOS

LIPSOI

Akköy

Selimiye

Yatağan

ALTINKUM

Milas

LÉROS

TURGUTREIS

TORBA

KÁLIMNOS

BODRUM

Ören

COS

BITEZ

Marmaris

ASTIPÁLAIA

Datça

NISIROS

SÍMI

ÇEŞME

Port, marina and spa surrounded by a number of holiday complexes with good, safe, sandy beaches, full leisure facilities and boat trips to Greek island of Chios. Lively family resort.

KUŞADASI

One of the busiest resorts on the Aegean. A picturesque harbour town surrounded by extensive holiday development, close to many historic sites, including Ephesus. Excellent shopping and bustling nightlife.

ALTINKUM

Developing beach resort, set on large sandy bay with good water sports facilities. Relaxed nightlife centres on waterfront bars, restaurants and discos. See BEACHES 1.

BODRUM

With its castle and twin bays, one of Turkey's prettiest resorts. A major yachting centre and lively nightspot, very popular but relatively uncommercialized. Beaches are adequate, but tend to be gravelly. See BODRUM.

BITEZ

Pleasant beach resort set around wide bay with narrow beach. Good swimming, excellent windsurfing and reasonably lively nightlife. Only 10 km from Bodrum.

TURGUTREIS

Town with fishing harbour and good beach. Less crowded than Gümbet (see BEACHES 1*), and with more local colour. Boat trips available to beaches and islands around peninsula.*

TORBA

This relatively secluded village has an away-from-it-all atmosphere, but yet is only 7 km from Bodrum. There is no beach, but swimming and sunbathing can be enjoyed from wooden jetties. There are pleasant open-air restaurants and waterfront bars.

Mediterranean

MARMARIS
Beautiful harbour surrounded by pine-clad hills, with Turkey's biggest yacht marina. Lively cosmopolitan atmosphere. See MARMARIS.

DATÇA
Pretty little resort town set on mountainous peninsula. See MARMARIS-EXCURSION.

FETHIYE
Unspoilt harbour town with good market and waterfront restaurants. Nearest beach is Çalış at 7 km, but more popular is the beautiful, picture-postcard lagoon of Ölü Deniz, 12 km away. See BEACHES 2.

KAŞ
Pretty fishing village, with laid-back, Bohemian atmosphere, away from the big package-holiday crowds. Relaxed and romantic nightlife based around quayside restaurants and bars.

KEMER
New, purpose-built seaside resort, with modern holiday complexes of hotels, restaurants, bars, discos and marina set on spectacular, scenic coast. Beaches good but pebbly.

ANTALYA
Major city on Mediterranean coast, with picturesque old town. Not a great beach resort, but ideal sightseeing base. See ANTALYA.

SIDE
Seaside village clustered around the ruins of ancient Side; popular with young holiday-makers, and often packed out in summer. Lively bars and restaurants, and two sandy beaches. See BEACHES 2, HISTORICAL SITES 2.

ALANYA
Spectacular resort built at the foot of rocky hill capped with ruins of Selçuk fortress. Popular with Turks as well as tourists, it is a typical 'sunshine' resort, with good restaurants and lively nightlife. See Alanya.

Accidents & Breakdowns: If you have an accident you should report it to the police immediately, even if no-one has been hurt. Exchange insurance details and get a statement from the police. If the car is a write-off you will need a customs certificate from the nearest customs office in order to leave Turkey without the vehicle. On main roads you will rarely be more than two hours' drive from a service station. If you break down, telephone your car rental agency for assistance (Avis have 24-hr offices at İzmir, Dalaman and Antalya), or ask for help at the nearest village. If you have arranged breakdown cover with the AA or RAC, you will be able to get assistance from the TTOK (*Türkiye Turing ve Otomobil Kurumu* – Turkish Touring and Automobile Club), which has an office in İzmir, tel: 51-217149. Local garages will have no trouble repairing Fiats, Mercedes and Renaults, the most popular makes in Turkey, but there may be difficulty getting spares for other makes. However, Turkish mechanics are very ingenious and will usually manage to get you back on the road. See **Driving**.

Accommodation: Accommodation ranges from cheap family-run pensions which can be found just about anywhere, to top-class luxury hotels, confined to major cities like İzmir and Antalya. Most of the

Marmaris

accommodation in the region is in pensions (*pansiyon* in Turkish), self-catering apartments and middle-range hotels. The Ministry of Culture and Tourism divides hotels into five grades: L (Luxury), 1, 2, 3 and 4, but apart from L and 1 these are not a good indication of quality (for example, an otherwise excellent hotel would be graded low simply because it has no restaurant). The best approach is simply to choose a hotel or pension that catches your eye, and ask to see the room before you decide. Prices are displayed prominently beside the reception desk: for a basic double room in a pension, with shared shower and toilet facilities, expect to pay around £5-10. A double room with private WC and hand-held shower in one of the better pensions costs £8-20. A pleasant double room in a mid-range hotel, with private bathroom costs £10-30. Luxury hotels cost upwards of £50 a night. These prices can drop by as much as 20% outside the high season (May-September). Advance booking is strongly recommended for top and middle-range accommodation during the high season; except at the very busiest times (e.g. during festivals) you should always be able to find a room in a cheap pension, especially out of town.

Facilities in the cheaper accommodation are usually pretty basic: pegs or a rack to hang clothes on rather than a wardrobe; a hand-held show-

Kalkan

er and a drain in the floor rather than a proper shower tray; in some places you may find 'hole-in-the-floor' WCs which are flushed using the bucket of water provided. Hot water is often provided by a solar heater, which means that the best time for a shower is late afternoon or early evening. In some places a gas or wood-fired boiler is used, and you may have to pay extra for this (around 1500TL). See **Camping & Caravanning, Youth Hostels.**

Airports: Turkey's Aegean and Mediterranean coasts are served by three international airports: İzmir (Adnan Menderes), 10 km south of İzmir; Dalaman, about halfway between Marmaris and Fethiye; and Antalya. These airports are served mainly by charter flights from the UK; scheduled flights (mainly British Airways and Turkish Airlines (THY)) go from London to Istanbul, İzmir and Antalya. Package holiday visitors will be transferred by coach to their destination: from İzmir to Kuşadası (1 hr 15 min), Çeşme (1 hr 30 min), Altınkum (2 hr 30 min), Bodrum (4 hr); from Dalaman to Marmaris (2 hr), Datça (3 hr), Fethiye (2 hr), Kaş (3 hr 30 min); and from Antalya to Kemer (1 hr), Side (1 hr 20 min) and Alanya (2 hr). Independent travellers can use the bus service connecting the airport terminal with the city bus station at İzmir and Antalya; at Dalaman there are buses from the terminal to Marmaris or Fethiye. There is also a 24-hr taxi service at Dalaman (about £12 to Fethiye, £20 to Marmaris) and a car-rental desk. For flight information, contact the Turkish Airlines Information & Reservation Office: Büyük Efes Hotel, İzmir, tel: 51-141220; Dalaman Airport, tel: 6119-1899; Hastane Caddesi, Ozel Idare Ishani Alti, Antalya, tel: 311-112830; Em Air, Neyzen Tefvik Caddesi, Bodrum, tel: 6141-2100; Atatürk Caddesi 30/B, Marmaris, tel: 6121-13751. The Turkish Airlines office in the UK is at 11 Hanover Street, London W1, tel: 071-4999247. For information on British Airways flights, contact the BA desk at Istanbul Airport, tel: 1-5732920 and ask to be put through to British Airways.

Alanya: This is one of the prettiest resorts on Turkey's Mediterranean coast, with its palm-lined waterfront and Riviera atmosphere. It was a Selçuk stronghold in the 13thC, and the town's major sights date from this period. The hilltop fortress was built by the Selçuk sultan Alaeddin

Keykobat on a site that had been fortified since the 2ndC BC (0800-1900: 5000TL). Inside the walls, from which you can enjoy terrific views over town and sea, are a Byzantine church, a mosque, a caravanserai and a covered bazaar. At the northeast corner is the sinister spot once known as *adam atacagi* – 'the place from which men are thrown'. At the foot of the fortress hill, beside the harbour is the Kızıl Kule (Red Tower), which houses an ethnographic museum (0800-1200, 1330-1730: 2000TL), and the Tersane, a Selçuk shipyard. On the west side of the hill is Damlataş Cave (0900-1700: 1000TL), whose high humidity is said to be good for asthma sufferers. For the rest of us it is just plain sweaty, but the coloured stalactite formations are impressive, and worth seeing before the heat gets too much. See **BEACHES 2, RESORTS-MEDITERRANEAN**.

Anatolia: This is the name given to the Asian part of Turkey, the great landmass bounded by the Black Sea to the north, the Aegean to the west, and the Mediterranean to the south. The name comes from the Greek word *anatole*, meaning 'rising' (of the sun). In times past the region was known as Asia Minor.

Antalya: See **ANTALYA, MUSEUMS, RESORTS-MEDITERRANEAN**.

Antalya

Didyma

Aphrodisias: See APHRODISIAS, HISTORICAL SITES 1, KUŞADASI-EXCURSION 2.

Architecture: Knowing the meaning of the following terms will help you to appreciate the many archaeological sites in the region:

Acropolis – a fortified hilltop, where the inhabitants of a city took refuge when under attack.

Agora – market square and meeting place.

Amphora – two-handled container with pointed base, for storing wine or water.

Architrave – lintel or stone beam resting on top of columns.

Basilica – early Christian church, with a central hall flanked by side halls of lesser height.

Bouleuterion – meeting place for the city's legislative council; the ancient equivalent of the Town Hall.

Colonnade – a row of columns, usually lining a street.

Heroon – shrine dedicated to a deified hero.

Necropolis – literally, City of the Dead. A cemetery.

Odeum – a small, semicircular theatre, used for concerts and plays, debates, lectures and council meetings.

Propylon – the entrance gate to a temple or other sacred area.

Stoa – a small colonnade, not attached to a larger building.

Aspendus: See HISTORICAL SITES 2.

Atatürk (1880-1938): Kemal Atatürk was the statesman who, almost single-handedly, created modern Turkey. Born Mustafa Kemal, he took part in the Young Turk movement of 1908-9 that opposed the rule of the Sultan. He led the army that won the War of Independence against the invading Greeks in 1919-22, and became the first President of the new Republic of Turkey in 1923. The capital was moved to Ankara, and from there Kemal set about 'Europeanizing' the country with sweeping reforms. Islamic law was replaced with a secular legal system, women were given the vote, the Arabic script was replaced with a Latin-based alphabet and the education system was reformed. His foresight was responsible for the relatively high standard of living enjoyed by most Turks today. In 1934 he changed his name to Kemal Atatürk (literally 'Father of the Turks'), and today he is revered as a great national hero. Every town has its Atatürk statue on the main square, and at 0905 every 10 November, the anniversary of his death, the whole country comes to a halt for a moment of reflection, and car horns and sirens blare. See **KUŞADASI-EXCURSION 1**.

Banks: See **Money**.

Best Buys: Think Turkey and you think carpets. Turkish carpets are an excellent buy, though not cheap. There are carpet shops in every resort, many of them geared to the mass tourist trade. Better deals and

more fun are to be had hunting carpets in the bazaars and smaller shops. Turkish carpets can be made from wool or silk, and are made by knotting the yarn round two vertical warps, unlike Persian carpets which are knotted around a single warp. This results in a stronger, more durable carpet, which will easily outlive you to become a family heirloom. Things to look for: tightness of weave – the more knots per square centimetre, the more durable (and the more expensive) the carpet (this can range from 20-30 for a coarse wool carpet to 100-200 for the finest silk – around 4 to 5 million knots in the whole carpet!); fastness of dyes – wipe a wet, white handkerchief over a corner of the carpet, and if the colour comes off, artificial dyes have been used; also, spread the pile and look at the base – has the colour faded at the surface? Of course, in the end it is a combination of price and attractiveness that will make your decision for you. A less expensive, but no less attractive alternative to a carpet is a kilim, a small rug/wall-hanging that has been woven rather than knotted.

Copper and brass-ware are popular souvenirs. You will find many shops offering trays, pots, pans, boxes, lamps, coffee-pots, samovars, candlesticks – all kinds of things, and generally good value. Jewellery is another good buy. Gold is sold by weight (a sign posted in the bazaar, and updated daily, shows the current price), plus extra for workmanship. If you want sterling silver, look for the hallmark; there is plenty of cheaper nickel-silver ware around. Other handicrafts worth looking at are ceramics, alabaster, and meerschaum pipes and figurines.

Leather and suede can be a real bargain in Turkey, but shop around to find the best fit and workmanship (check seams, quality of stitching, etc.). Be wary of shops offering made-to-measure clothing that will be ready in 24 hours; it may well fall apart in 24 hours too. Embroidered headscarves and blouses are also good value.

If you want to take home a taste of Turkey, you will find stalls everywhere selling Turkish Delight (*lokum* in Turkish) in a variety of flavours, and a vast range of cheap fresh spices, herbs and scented teas. Around Marmaris you can buy delicious, locally produced, pine-scented honey (*çam balı*). See **Markets**, **Shopping.**

Bicycle & Motorcycle Hire: Mopeds and bicycles can be hired from a number of rental agencies in most coastal resorts. You will need your driving licence to hire a moped, and some form of deposit: either cash, or perhaps leaving your licence with the rental agency.

Bodrum: See BODRUM, RESORTS-AEGEAN.

Budget:

Hotel breakfast	5000-10,000TL
Lunch	5000-20,000TL
Lahmacun (Turkish pizza)	1000-2000TL
Dinner	10,000-30,000TL
Museum entry	1000-10,000TL
Glass of tea, coffee	500-1000TL
House wine	5000-10,000TL
Bottle of beer	1500-3000TL
Soft drink	1000TL
Bottle of *raki*	15,000TL

Buses: The bus is the cheapest and best way to travel in Turkey. Private companies operate an extensive network of frequent services between all cities and towns, large and small. On many routes however, there is no set timetable, so it is best to visit the bus station (*otogar* in large towns, main square in villages) and check out fares and departure times a day or two before you go. Prices are posted at the ticket office, and are often ridiculously low – on average about £1 per 100 km. On busy routes, buy your ticket in advance as the bus service is very popular. Buses are generally comfortable, though often plagued with cigarette smoke. Small bottles of mineral water are available for no extra charge. If your destination is a large town, then there will usually be a free minibus service to shuttle passengers from the *otogar* on the outskirts to the town centre (you must show your bus ticket).

Byzantium: See **History.**

Camping & Caravanning: Good quality camp sites are still thin on the ground in Turkey. The best are those registered with the Ministry of Culture and Tourism (a list of registered sites can be obtained from the Tourism and Information Office in London, and especially those run by the Mocamp Kervansaray chain). These are clean and well-maintained, with toilets, showers, kitchen, laundry, shop and electrical hook-up. There are registered sites at or near Alanya, Kuşadası, İzmir, Datça, Marmaris, Bodrum and Fethiye. See **Tourist Information.**

Car Hire: Hiring a car is a good way to see more of the region. There are rental agencies in all main towns. Avis is the most widespread of the major companies, with offices at İzmir, Dalaman and Antalya airports, and in Alanya, Antalya, Bodrum, Çeşme, İzmir, Kaş, Kemer, Kuşadası, Marmaris and Side. Vehicles range from a Fiat 124 (known as a Murat in Turkey) to Renault 12, Fiat 131 and Suzuki 4WD jeeps. You will need your driving licence (an International Driving Permit is recommended). Minimum age varies among companies, but is generally 21 or 25. A cash deposit will be required if you are not paying by credit card, and an additional petrol deposit of 50,000TL may be charged, which is refunded if you return the car with a full tank (or whatever was in it when you picked it up – check this before you drive off). Car hire can be expensive – around £200-250 a week for unlimited mileage, not including petrol. Make sure that quoted prices include insurance. It is best to arrange and pay for car hire in the UK before you leave; this is easily done through a travel agent. The least expensive way to hire a car is to take a fly-drive package from a tour operator; these offer a car for as little as £150 a week unlimited mileage. See **Accidents and Breakdowns**, **Driving.**

Castle of St. Peter: See BODRUM-WALK, WHAT TO SEE.

Chemists: In Turkish, *eczane* or *eczanesi*. Chemists are open during normal shop hours. A rota system will be in operation, so that there is always one chemist open all night and at weekends. The schedule of late openings will be displayed on the door of the shop; otherwise, tel: 011 to find out which chemist is on duty.

Climate: The Aegean and Mediterranean coasts of Turkey enjoy hot, sunny summers and mild winters. Average summer temperatures (June-September) are 23-31°C, water temperature 24-29°C. Spring and autumn are pleasant times to visit, especially for sightseeing, as the heat is less intense, with temperatures of 16-23°C, but there is still plenty of sunshine. Sea temperatures in October and November are still high, around 20-25°C in the Mediterranean. Most of the year's rain falls in January and February, and winter temperatures average 9-12°C.

Cnidus: See MARMARIS-EXCURSION, WHAT TO SEE.

Complaints: If you feel you have been overcharged, or are dissatisfied with any aspect of service in a hotel or restaurant, complain either to the manager of the establishment, or to your courier if you are on a package holiday.

Consulates:

UK	Şehit Ersan Cad. 46/A, Cankaya, Ankara, tel: 4-1274310.
Australia	Nenehatun Cad. 83, Gaziosmanpaşa, Ankara, tel: 4-1286715.
Canada	Nenehatun Cad. 75, Gaziosmanpaşa, Ankara, tel: 4-1361275.
USA	Atatürk Bulv. 110, Kavaklidere, Ankara, tel: 4-1265470.

Conversion Charts:

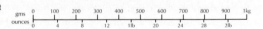

Credit Cards: See Money.

Crime & Theft: Turkey is in general a safe country for tourists, with a low crime rate, but it makes sense to take the usual precautions against theft. Leave valuables in the hotel safe and not in your room (or carry them with you). Beware of pickpockets in crowded areas like bazaars. Report any theft to the police immediately. See **Police**.

Currency: The unit of currency is the *Türk Lirası,* or Turkish lira (TL). Banknotes are issued in denominations of 10,000TL, 5000TL, 1000TL, 500TL, 100TL, 50TL and 20TL. Coins are rare, but you may see some of 5TL, 10TL, 20TL and 50TL. Inflation is high, in the region of 30%, but regular devaluation of the lira against foreign currency keeps prices in Sterling fairly level. See **Money**.

Customs: The Turks are a very friendly, polite and hospitable people, and will always be ready to strike up a conversation if they can speak your language (and sometimes even if they can't!). Good manners are

very important to them, and although in big cities and popular holiday resorts they are very tolerant of the ways of visitors, there are some points of etiquette you should bear in mind, especially in smaller villages and in country areas: avoid kissing and cuddling in public; don't point your finger or your foot at someone (this is considered rude); avoid blowing your nose in a public place (turn away, or go into a public toilet); do not make jokes about the muezzin's call to prayer, Atatürk or the Turkish flag. Mosques are open to non-Muslims, but not when prayers are taking place. Dress conservatively to visit a mosque – long trousers or skirt below the knees, long-sleeved shirt or blouse, headscarf for women – and remove shoes before entering.

Turkish body language may cause some confusion. Shaking your head means 'I don't understand', not 'no'. A Turk indicates 'no' by tilting his head up and back, and raising his eyebrows. This may be accompanied by a click of the tongue, or the word *yok* or *hayir*. 'Yes' is a forward nod of the head. 'Come with me' is a downward sweep of the hand, not the beckoning finger of the British.

Women travelling alone, especially in more remote areas, may be subject to cat-calls and unwanted approaches. It is advisable to avoid wearing revealing clothes, and if possible travel with a companion. Note that the village coffee-house is essentially a male preserve (the Turkish equivalent of the local pub) and women are not welcome there.

Customs Allowances:

Duty Paid Into:	Cigarettes	*or*	Cigars	*or*	Tobacco	Spirits		Wine
Turkey	400		50		200g	5 *l*		None
U.K.	200		50		250g	1 *l*	*or*	2 *l*

Medusa

Didyma: Connected to Miletus (see **A–Z**) by the Sacred Way, this great Temple of Apollo was one of the greatest monuments of ancient times. People came here from far and wide to consult the oracle. The stumps of the huge columns impart something of the feeling of awe that the supplicants must have felt 2000 years ago. Lying on the grass beside the entrance is the giant, carved head of the Medusa, which came from a frieze which once adorned part of the architraves. See **HISTORICAL SITES 1**.

Dolmuş: These are minibuses that provide transport over short distances in and around towns and between villages. The fare and destination of each is displayed in the front window. There is no timetable; you just climb in, and the driver leaves when all the seats are full (*dolmuş* means 'filled' or 'stuffed' in Turkish – which is how they often feel!). Pay your fare to the driver on boarding or when you leave. You can get off anywhere on the route by shouting '*Musait yerde!*' (mew-sah-yeet yer-deh), meaning 'This is the place!', and pay only a proportion of the full fare (ask beforehand how much it is to your destination – sometimes you will have to pay the full fare anyway). See **Buses, Transport**.

Drinks: The most popular local drink is tea (*çay*), served Turkish-style in little tulip-shaped glasses, with sugar lumps to taste, but no milk. A pleasant variation is apple tea. Coffee (*kahve*) is served very strong, black and sweet, with a thick sludge of grounds at the bottom of the cup. Mineral water (*maden suyu*) is widely available, and preferable to tap water (quite safe to drink, but sometimes tastes unpleasant). *Ayran* is a sharp, refreshing drink made by diluting yoghurt with mineral water. Although Turkey is a Muslim country, alcoholic drinks are widely available. The national alcoholic drink is *raki*, a strong, anise-type liquor similar to Greek ouzo, usually mixed half-and-half with water. Locally produced wines (Tekel, Doluca, Kavaklıdere) are cheap and surprisingly good. The most widespread beers are Tuborg and the Turkish-brewed Efes Pilsen. Cold soft drinks and mineral water are on sale from stalls in towns, at beaches, in museums and at most tourist attractions. See **Eating Out**, **Food**.

Driving: A car is an excellent way of seeing the Turkish coast. Hiring is better than bringing your own car, as the drive is long (London to İzmir is 3700 km, London to Antalya nearly 4000 km – a good five days' driving). To bring a car into Turkey you require an International Driving Permit (£3 from AA or RAC), a Green Card insurance certificate endorsed for both Europe and Asia, and a transit visa for Bulgaria which you pass through on the way. All cars must carry a nationality sticker, a first-aid kit and two red warning triangles. For full details of requirements, contact the AA or RAC.

Driving is on the right, seat-belts are compulsory and speed limits are 50 kph in built-up areas, 90 kph elsewhere. The legal blood alcohol limit for driving is *zero*. Regulations and road signs are similar to the rest of Europe. Some important Turkish words you will see on road signs: *yavaz* – slow; *dur* – stop; *dikkat* – caution; *centrum* or *sehir merkezi* – town centre. Petrol is widely available on the main roads, and costs around 1200TL a litre. Main roads are generally in good condition, and driving is quite pleasant outside cities and large towns. Minor roads may be in very poor condition. All main roads are plagued by convoys of smoky, oil-dripping, slow-moving lorries, which can become frustrating. Driving at night is not recommended because of the lack of road markings, and the danger of hitting unlit tractors, pedestrians and animals.

The traffic police (*trafik polisi*, dark green uniforms with white caps) regularly wave down traffic at checkpoints to check documents and vehicle condition. The purpose of this is mainly to catch local people driving without insurance or with cars in a dangerous condition. As a foreigner you will often be waved on, but occasionally you will be asked to show passport, licence, insurance, etc., and maybe to check that lights, horn, wipers, etc. are in working order. See **Accidents & Breakdowns**, **Car Hire**.

Drugs: The import, export, possession or use of narcotic is strictly forbidden, and penalties for offenders are severe.

Eating Out: You will never be stuck for somewhere to eat in Turkey. There are eating places everywhere, usually open from early morning until late at night. The most 'upmarket' place to eat is in a *restoran* or *lokanta*, with waiter service and full lunch and dinner menu. Then there is the *hazir yemek* (literally 'ready food'), which has a selection of ready-prepared dishes to choose from. *Kebapcı* and *köftecı* serve a

familiar selection of shish and doner kebabs, meatballs and other grilled dishes, while a *pideci* serves pitta bread with a variety of fillings. A *bufe* is a snack-bar or street-stall selling sandwiches and pastries, and a *kuru yemis* sells dried fruit and nuts. The best places to eat, in terms of both value and atmosphere, are small family-run *lokantas*. In the more expensive places you tend to be paying for surroundings or prime position (e.g. harbour-side) rather than better quality food or service. In any restaurant you will be invited to look at the dishes available, either in the kitchen or in a counter display, and make your choice there. Menus are used only in Western-style and tourist restaurants (although most restaurants have a price list posted outside). In popular tourist areas, most waiters will speak enough English for you to get by; otherwise, just point at what you want! Order dishes as you want them, not all in one go, i.e. wait until you've finished your starter before ordering a main course, otherwise it will all come at once. Note that it is not unusual for food to be served lukewarm; this is because the Turks enjoy spinning out their mealtimes with talk and laughter, and the food is often cold anyway by the time they finish eating it! If you want it piping hot, say so. In the topics section of this guide, 'Inexpensive' means that dinner, excluding drinks, costs less than 15,000TL; 'Moderate' means 15,000-30,000TL; and 'Expensive' means over 30,000TL. See **RESTAURANTS-ANTALYA, BODRUM, KUŞADASI, MARMARIS, Food**.

Electricity: 220 V/50HzAC. Plugs are European round two-pin type, but there are two sizes in use. Buy a suitable adaptor before you leave, or else stick to battery-powered appliances.

Ephesus: This was one of the most important of ancient cities, founded around the 10thC BC by Ionian Greeks. It was a major trading port, and a centre for the cult of Artemis, the virgin huntress and goddess of the moon. The Greek Artemis assimilated the much older cult of Cybele, the many-breasted Earth Mother of Anatolia, and worship was focussed on the Temple of Artemis (see **KUŞADASI-WHAT TO SEE**), built in the 4th-3rdC BC, one of the Seven Wonders of the Ancient World. At its height the city had a population of 200,000, and much of its splendour remains to be enjoyed today. See **EPHESUS, HISTORICAL SITES 1**.

Earth Mother

Events:

January: Camel-wrestling Festival, Selçuk and Aydın.

March-April: Mesir Festival, Manisa, when a traditional local restorative is brewed and distributed.

April-May: Ephesus Festival of Culture and Art, Selçuk.

May: International Festival, Bergama, events in the theatre on the acropolis, folk music, dancing; Pamukkale Theatre Festival, Denizli.

June: Festival of Art and Tourism, Marmaris, concerts, exhibitions, folk dancing; International Mediterranean Festival, İzmir.

July: Pop Music Festival, Kuşadası; Sea Festival, Çeşme; Folklore and Water Sports Festival, Foca.

August-September: International Fair, İzmir.

September: Art and Culture Week, Bodrum, concerts, art exhibitions.

October: International Film and Art Festival, Antalya.

December: St. Nicholas Festival, Demre, special services in 4thC AD Church of Father Christmas (see **Noel Baba Kilisesi**).

Food: Turkish cuisine is a delicious and intriguing blend of Mediterranean and Middle Eastern influences, and is rated by gourmets as being on a par with French and Chinese. Great importance is placed on the use of the freshest ingredients: fish (*balık*), meat (*etli*) – lamb, chicken and beef (Muslims are not allowed to eat pork) – aubergines (*patlıcan*), peppers (*biber*), tomatoes (*domates*), beans (*fasulye*). Staples

are rice (*pilav*), cracked wheat (*bulgur*), potatoes (*patates*) and fresh, crusty bread (*ekmek*). Most meals begin with *mezes*, a selection of appetizers, which may include various salads, *cacık* (yoghurt with garlic and grated cucumber), *börek* (pastry rolls filled with goat's cheese), cold stuffed peppers and aubergines, *kalamar* (battered, deep-fried squid), *yaprak dolması* (stuffed vine leaves) and *cerkez tavuğu* (minced chicken flavoured with walnuts). Main courses can be grilled meats: *şiş kebap* is small chunks of marinated lamb grilled on skewers, *şiş köfte* is grilled meatballs of minced lamb, *çöp şiş* is tiny morsels of lamb grilled on wooden skewers; or casseroles of lamb or beef, accompanied by a couple of vegetable dishes; or delicious local fish, especially *trança* (tuna), *kılıç* (swordfish), *mercan* (red coralfish), *levrek* (sea bass), *kalkan* (turbot) and *sardalya* (sardines). Desserts are invariably sweet and sticky, like *baklava* (flaky pastry and groundnut soaked in syrup), and *sutlaç* (rice-pudding). Alternatively, you can ask for *dondurma* (ice-cream) or *meyva* (fresh fruit).

Breakfast generally consists of fresh bread with honey, jam or cheese, and perhaps some olives or a boiled egg, washed down with tea. Turkish coffee is generally only drunk in the evening after dinner. See **RESTAURANTS-ANTALYA, BODRUM, KUŞADASI, MARMARIS, Eating Out**.

Guides: Organized coach tours generally include a professional guide to take you round the archaeological sites. If you are not on a tour, you can arrange for a guide through the local Tourist Office. At some of the quieter sites, off the main tourist trail, the site guardian will often give you a guided tour for a small fee. See **Tourist Information**, **Tours.**

Gulet: See **Yachting.**

Health: Turkey has good quality medical and dental services, though not quite up to British standards. You will have to pay on the spot. Make sure you get a receipt so you can claim it back from your holiday insurance. There are state hospitals and Red Crescent clinics (Turkish equivalent of Red Cross) which are relatively cheap, and private doctors and clinics who are more expensive. Your hotel should be able to recommend an English-speaking doctor or dentist. For a list of doctors, dentists, hospitals and clinics in your area, consult the local Yellow Pages (*Altın Rehber*), which has an abbreviated index in English. For minor complaints, ask for advice at a chemist (see **A–Z**).

No vaccinations are required for this region of Turkey, but if you are going to be visiting the remoter areas of eastern Turkey, you should consider approaching your doctor for anti-malarial pills, and inoculations against typhoid, cholera and polio. Standards of hygiene in popular tourist areas are high, and the tap-water is safe to drink everywhere (though mineral water tastes nicer!). Avoid obviously dirty restaurants, and wash or peel fruit before eating it. Beware of sunburn – take a sun-hat and a good blocking cream, and don't overdo the sunbathing on the first few days. See **Insurance**.

Hierapolis: See KUŞADASI-EXCURSION 2, MUSEUMS.

History: The Aegean and Mediterranean shores of Turkey are steeped in history, and have seen the rise and fall of many empires. Archaeological finds date back as far as 10,000 BC, but the first known civilization in Turkey is that of the Hittites, who flourished c.1450-1200 BC and controlled central Anatolia (see **A-Z**) and much of Syria. After the fall of Troy c.1260 BC, Greeks began to migrate to the Aegean shores of Anatolia, and the following period saw the rise of Greek culture and the growth of cities like Miletus (see **A–Z**), which established colonies as far away as the shores of the Black Sea. In 546 BC the whole of Asia Minor, including the Greek cities on the west coast, came under Persian control. Then in 334 BC Alexander the Great crossed from Macedonia and in one mighty campaign conquered the whole of Asia Minor and the Middle East. After his death in 323 BC his empire was split up, and several small city-states flourished, among them Pergamum, which dominated western Asia Minor in the 2ndC BC. In 133 BC the last King of Pergamum bequeathed his kingdom to the Roman Empire, and a few years later the whole region came under Roman rule as the province of Asia. The coming of Christianity had a profound effect on the region, and of course on the Roman Empire as a whole. The apostle Paul made his famous missionary journeys to Asia Minor in AD 40-56. In 392 Christianity became the state religion, and in 395 the Roman Empire was divided. The eastern part, known as the Byzantine Empire, had its capital at Byzantium (on the site of present-day Istanbul), which was renamed Constantinople after the Emperor

Constantine. As the western Roman Empire declined, Byzantium prospered, reaching its zenith in the 6thC AD under Justinian the Great,
when it controlled all of Anatolia, the Balkans and much of north
Africa. The Byzantines were threatened by the Arabs after the rise of

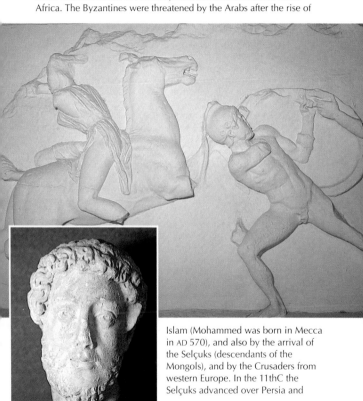

Islam (Mohammed was born in Mecca
in AD 570), and also by the arrival of
the Selçuks (descendants of the
Mongols), and by the Crusaders from
western Europe. In the 11thC the
Selçuks advanced over Persia and

Anatolia, and in 1204 the Crusaders sacked Constantinople. The Byzantine Empire disintegrated. Meanwhile, the powerful Osmanli family had united many of the small emirates which had sprung up in Anatolia after the Selçuk invasion, and began to build their own empire, the Ottoman Empire. In 1453 the Ottomans took Constantinople and made it their capital, renaming it Istanbul. The Ottomans ruled Turkey for over 400 years. At its peak, under Sultan Suleyman the Magnificent in the 16thC, the Ottoman Empire stretched from Hungary to north Africa. But in the 18th and 19thC decline set in. In the First World War the Ottoman Empire sided with Germany and was defeated. The empire was divided under the Treaty of Sevres. The Greek army invaded in 1919, but was repulsed by the Turks under the leadership of Kemal Atatürk (see **A–Z**). On 29 October 1923, the modern Republic of Turkey (*Türkiye Cumhuriyeti*) was established, with Atatürk as its first President.

Insurance: You are strongly advised to take out adequate travel and medical insurance before your trip. Your travel agent will be able to advise you of the most suitable policy. See **Accidents & Breakdowns**, **Crime & Theft**, **Health**.

İzmir: İzmir is a thoroughly modern Turkish city, the third largest in the country, sprawled around its beautiful bay. But beneath the modern facade lies a rich history. This is the ancient city of Smyrna, famed as the birthplace of Homer, fought over through the centuries by Greeks, Turks, Byzantines, Genoese, Selçuks, Ottomans, Crusaders and Arabs. Its known history dates from the 3rd millenium BC, but its rise to prominence began following its re-establishment by Alexander the Great in the 4thC BC, when he built a fortress on top of Mount Pagus (Kadifekale). Under Greek and Roman rule the city prospered as one of the principal centres of Mediterranean trade, and so it has remained until modern times. Many European merchants made their homes here, and the Turks came to call the place Giaour İzmir, or 'Infidel Smyrna'. The city has been repeatedly ravaged by fires and earthquakes throughout its history, most recently at the end of the 1921-2 war between Greece and Turkey, when the retreating Greeks set fire to the town as they were routed by the army of Kemal Atatürk (see **A–Z**). As a result, most of the city you see today is relatively new and sophisticated, but there are still plenty of interesting sights. See KUŞADASI-EXCURSION 1.

Kekova Island: Accessible by boat from Kaş. Boat trips generally include visits to the sites of ancient Aperlae and Teimeiussa. Around the coast and at the island, you can see the submerged remains of the flooded cities through the crystal-clear water, with walls and tombs occasionally rising eerily above the surface.

Kuşadası: See KUŞADASI, RESORTS-AEGEAN.

Laundries: The popular resorts have a laundry or two offering service washes and dry-cleaning services. There are no coin-operated laundries. Check the local Yellow Pages (*Altın Rehber*). Hotel laundries tend to be expensive.

Lost Property: Any loss should be reported to the police. See **Insurance**, **Police**.

Manisa: This pleasant town 40 km east of İzmir is the site of ancient Magnesia ad Sipylum, which was briefly capital of the Byzantine Empire in the early 13thC, when Constantinople was occupied by the Crusaders. Sights include two great Ottoman monuments: the Muradiye Camii (Murat Mosque) built 1583-6, and the Ülü Camii (Great Mosque) built in 1366. There is a fine museum beside the Murat Mosque (Tue.-Sun. 0900-1700: 2000TL).

Markets: Every Turkish town has its market (*carsi*) where farmers and vendors from the surrounding villages come to offer their goods. These are good places to buy inexpensive fresh food, and to hunt for bargains in clothing, fabrics and household goods. Market days vary from town to town. Ask at the local Tourist Information Office. See **Best Buys**.

Marmaris: See MARMARIS.

Meryemana: See KUŞADASI-WHAT TO SEE.

Miletus: This important ancient city lies on the south edge of the plain of the River Maeander (once an inlet of the sea, before the river filled it with silt), facing Priene (see **A–Z**) to the north. The settlement probably dates from the 10thC BC, though the main ruins you see today are from the Roman period. The city was laid out on a grid plan devised by the local architect, Hippodamus, though few traces of it remain. The principal structures are the great theatre, capped by the ruins of a Byzantine fortress; the Baths of Faustina; the bouleuterion; and the nymphaeum (fountain). East of the north agora are the remains of a Selçuk bathhouse built on the foundations of a Roman baths. Unlike its neighbour Priene, this site has a rather bleak and desolate atmosphere, and having once seen the ruins, you will probably not want to linger. There is a small museum on the approach road, and drinks stalls beside the car park (Museum 0830-1230, 1330-1730: 2000TL). See HISTORICAL SITES 1, **Didyma**.

Money: You will find banks in the town centres of most resorts. They are open 0900-1200, 1330-1700 Mon.-Fri. Popular resorts also have many exchange offices, which stay open 0900-0000 seven days a week in summer. To cash traveller's cheques you will need your passport. Most types will be accepted, but stick to the big names like Thomas Cook and American Express and you won't go wrong. Large hotels may also cash traveller's cheques, but banks give the best rate of exchange. Don't buy a lot of Turkish lira in Britain before you leave, as you will get a much better rate of exchange once you are in Turkey. Remember to hang on to your exchange receipts. Eurocheques can be cashed at most banks. Credit cards are generally accepted only by large hotels, expensive tourist shops and restaurants, and car rental agencies. See **Crime & Theft**, **Currency**.

Newspapers: The English-language daily, *The Turkish Daily News,* is available from most newsagents for 900TL, and covers Turkish and international news. British newspapers, one or two days late, can be found at newsagents in popular resorts like Kuşadası, Bodrum, Marmaris, etc., but are expensive at around 6800TL. The *International Herald Tribune* is somewhat less expensive at 3200TL. See **What's On**.

Miletus

Nightlife: All the main holiday resorts offer Western-style discos, which stay open until the small hours, usually at the large package-tour hotels and holiday villages. These are much the same wherever you go, though the Club Akdeniz, Kuşadası, the Halikarnas, Bodrum, and the Talya Hotel Nightclub, Antalya, are above average. More intimate, and usually more fun, are the many bars that line the waterfront in resorts big and small, some with live music, some with taped music, some with no music, but all with a lively hubbub of conversation, and usually a mixed crowd of visitors and friendly locals. Take your pick! Big hotels and holiday villages often have dinner-shows including belly-dancing, but these are usually pure titillation and have little to do with traditional Turkish culture. Folk music and dancing are best seen during one of the many festivals. See **Events**.

Noel Baba Kilisesi (Church of Father Christmas): Believe it or not, the origins of Santa Claus are to be found, not in Lapland or Greenland, but in the village of Demre, which is about 40 km east of Kaş. St. Nicholas was born in this village in c. AD 300, and became the Bishop of Myra. He became the patron saint of children as a result of his many acts of generosity. According to tradition, one of these good deeds was to give three bags of gold to the three daughters of a poor family to pay their marriage dowries, and thus save them from taking to the streets as they would otherwise have had to do. So that he would remain anonymous, he dropped the bags of gold down the chimney during the night. The church here is very old, and has been subject to many additions and alterations, but it is thought that there has been a church on this site since the 3rd or 4thC AD; it is currently undergoing restoration work (0900-1700: 5000TL). Inside is the tomb of St. Nicholas (some of his bones can be seen in the museum at Antalya – see **MUSEUMS**), and in the garden outside is a statue of the saint as Father Christmas. The site of ancient Myra is nearby (see **HISTORICAL SITES 2**). See **Events**.

Ölü Deniz: See **BEACHES 2**.

Olympus: See **OLYMPUS**.

Opening Hours: These are general opening times, and may be subject to variation. For example, in popular tourist resorts, shops stay open until late in the evening, seven days a week.
Banks – 0900-1200, 1330-1700 Mon.-Fri. Closed Sat. & Sun.
Currency exchange offices – 0900-0000 daily, in summer.
Government offices – 0900-1700 Mon.-Fri. Closed Sat. & Sun.
Post offices – 0900-1700 Mon.-Fri. Closed Sat. & Sun. In large towns, often 24 hours, 7 days a week.
Shops – 0900-1700 Mon.-Sat. Closed Sun.

Orientation: The local Tourist Information Office will usually be able to provide a map of your resort and the surrounding area. A good road-touring map of Turkey is produced by Hallwag; it includes useful tourist information, and has street plans of Istanbul, İzmir, Kuşadası, Bodrum, Marmaris, Antalya and Alanya. Note that postal addresses in Turkey are written with the street name first then the number (e.g. Atatürk Cad. 110). If the building is on a side street, then the name of the main street is given first, then the side street, then the number (e.g. Atatürk Cad., Eski Banka Sokak 23). Turkish words for streets are: *Caddesi/Cad.* – Avenue; *Bulvarı/Bulv.* – Boulevard; *Sokak/Sok.* – Street.

Ottoman: See **History**.

Pamukkale: See KUŞADASI-EXCURSION 2.

Patara: 50 km northwest of Kaş (see **RESORTS-MEDITERRANEAN**) is a beautiful beach, backed by the ruins of ancient Patara (All times: 2000TL for car park). Climb the hill above the sand-filled theatre to find a deep cistern and the remains of what may have been an ancient lighthouse. There are lovely views over the ruined city and along Patara beach. See **BEACHES 2**.

Passports & Customs: British passport holders require a visa for visits to Turkey. These can be obtained by applying to the Turkish Consulate General, Rutland Lodge, Rutland Gardens, London SW7, tel: 071-5890360/0949. Apply in good time, as the application may take a few days to process. Health or vaccination certificates are not required. There is no limit on the amount of foreign currency you can take into the country. On departure you may take out no more than US$1000 worth of Turkish lira and foreign currency not exceeding the amount you brought in. Always keep your exchange receipts, as you will need them if you want to change any extra local currency before you leave. It is illegal to purchase or export antiquities. See **Customs Allowances**.

Pergamum: The ancient city of Pergamum flourished from 3rdC BC-2ndC AD, and reached the peak of its power under King Eumenes II (197-160 BC). It was here that a writing material made from animal hides, *pergamena*, was invented, later known as parchment. It was a great centre of art, learning and medicine. The city is mentioned in the Bible as one of the seven churches of Asia (Revelation 1:11). See **HISTORICAL SITES 1**, KUŞADASI-EXCURSION 3.

Perge: This city was visited by the Apostles Paul and Barnabas on their first missionary journey. Here you can explore the well-preserved theatre and stadium, and wander through the baths, following in the footsteps of the ancient Pergeans from the palaestra (exercise area) through the frigidarium, tepidarium and caldarium (cold, tepid and hot pools), before strolling down the colonnaded main street, with its ornamental water channel down the middle, fed by the fountain at the base of the acropolis. There are helpful interpretive notice boards dotted about the site, which explain what many of the ruins are and how they were used. See **HISTORICAL SITES 2**.

Photography: Stock up on film before you leave home, as it is more expensive in Turkey. If you do run out, major brands are on sale in most resorts. Protect film and cameras from the effects of heat – don't leave them in a parked car, or exposed to direct sunlight. If you want to take pictures of local people, it is good manners to ask permission first. Men and children are usually all too keen to pose, but in country areas it may be unwise to try to photograph women. It is forbidden to take pictures near military installations (e.g. beside the Asclepieum at Pergamum), inside most museums, and at active archaeological excavations (e.g. parts of Aphrodisias). If you want to take pictures inside a mosque, be discreet and do not use a flash.

Police: There are three kinds of police. The *jandarma* are drawn from the army, have military uniforms with red armbands and steel helmets, and it is their job to keep the peace, catch criminals, etc. Even the smallest village has its *jandarma* post. The *polis* wear dark green uniforms and white caps and drive around in black and white Renault 12s. Their job is to patrol highways, catch traffic offenders, and carry out general police duties in towns and cities. The *belediye zabitasi* wear blue uniforms, and are really weights and measures inspectors. They patrol markets and bazaars making sure that shopkeepers don't try to cheat customers. Emergency police numbers are given at the front of telephone directories, but there is little point in using them unless you speak fluent Turkish. If you need the services of the police (for road accidents, minor theft, etc., it is the *polis* you want), ask a local to call them for you, or go to the nearest police station yourself and try to find an officer who speaks some English. See **Crime & Theft**.

Post Offices: These are indicated by yellow signs marked PTT. They provide letter and parcel mail, local and international telephones, telegrams, sale of telephone tokens (*jetons*) and cards. All are open 0900-1700 Mon.-Fri. Main post offices in cities and major resorts (Kuşadası, Bodrum, Marmaris, Antalya) are open 24 hours, seven days a week. You will soon find that the staff in post offices are often curt, and sometimes downright rude. Cost of a stamp for a postcard to the UK is 800TL. Letter boxes are painted yellow. See **Telephones & Telegrams**.

Priene: Beautifully sited above the plain of the River Maeander, this ancient city was laid out on the grid system devised by Hippodamus of Miletus (see **A–Z**), with east-west main streets intersected at right angles by narrower alleys and stairways. The highlights include the theatre, dating from the 4thC BC, and the Temple of Athena (4th-2ndC BC), whose construction was paid for by Alexander the Great. Above all, the lovely setting makes Priene the ideal spot to enjoy an early evening stroll. See **HISTORICAL SITES 1**.

Public Holidays: Official holidays: 1 Jan. (New Year's Day); 23 April (National Independence & Children's Day); 19 May (Atatürk's Birthday, Youth & Sports Day); 30 Aug. (Victory Day); 29 Oct. (Republic Day). There are two major Islamic religious holidays, each lasting three to five days, and determined by the lunar calendar; this means they take place a week or two earlier each year. First is the Feast of Ramazan, which marks the end of the holy month of Ramazan, when Muslims must abstain from eating, drinking, smoking and sex between sunrise and sunset (mid-April 1991); and second is the Feast of Sacrifice, the most important holiday of the year, when millions of sheep are slaughtered for the festival (late June 1991).

Sardis: About 50 km east of İzmir (0900-1730: 2000TL). This ancient city was the 6thC BC seat of King Croesus, and it was here that coinage was invented. The coins were minted of local gold and silver, and the vast wealth that was thus accumulated in the city gave rise to the saying 'as rich as Croesus'. The impressive ruins include a gymnasium complex, part of which was converted to a synagogue in the 3rdC AD, a street of Byzantine shops and the Temple of Artemis.

Selçuk: See **History**.

Shopping: Shops generally open 0900-1900 Mon.-Sat., closed Sun., but shops catering to tourists are open from early morning until late in the evening, seven days a week. The most interesting places to shop are in the markets and bazaars which are found in every town. Here good-natured haggling is the norm: ask the price of whatever you want to buy, and if you are serious about buying it, offer half to two-thirds of the asking price, then haggle until you settle on a price somewhere in between. The seller may offer you a glass of tea while he discusses the merits of his goods, and you can accept without feeling obliged to buy. But remember not to make a firm offer unless you are serious; to settle on a price and then not buy is considered bad manners. Some vendors will name a price and say it is their 'best price'. Many genuinely mean this is the lowest price they will accept, and offer it so as to encourage Western tourists who may not feel comfortable with haggling. The only

way to find out if he is offering a good price is to shop around first, asking the price of similar articles elsewhere. If it seems a good price, you can come back to him later. In many tourist areas, fixed prices are becoming more common. If something is marked with a certain price, then that is the price, full stop; no haggling. Credit cards are only accepted in shops dealing in more expensive goods like carpets and leather – look for shops that display credit card signs. VAT (KDV in Turkish) is included in the price of many goods, and if you are buying something expensive – a carpet, say – it may be worth asking the shop for a KDV Refund Receipt, which can be cashed in at the exchange desk in the international departure lounge at the airport. Note that it is illegal to buy or export an antiquity, so do not be tempted by the boys who hang around the popular archaeological sites offering old coins and other objects for sale. They are almost all worthless fakes; and if they aren't, then you're breaking the law in buying them. See **Best Buys**.

Side: See BEACHES 2, HISTORICAL SITES 2, RESORTS-MEDITERRANEAN.

Smyrna: See KUŞADASI-EXCURSION 1, İzmir.

Sports: Turkey's coast is ideal for all kinds of water sports. Beginners and experts alike can indulge in windsurfing, water-skiing, parascending and dinghy sailing at all the major resorts. Instruction is available, and equipment can be hired. Scuba-diving is excellent, and can be organized through package operators (courses of instruction can be arranged). Diving equipment can be hired and air-tanks filled at major resorts like Bodrum and Marmaris. Tennis, mini-golf, table-tennis, volleyball, etc. can be enjoyed at the large hotels and holiday villages. Angling, both sea and freshwater is very good, and usually does not require a permit. For further information on any of these sports, contact the Turkish Tourism and Information Office in London (see **Tourist Information**). Unusual spectator sports include oiled wrestling (*yağlı güreş*) in which the contestants, wearing only leather breeches, and liberally smeared with oil from neck to toes, grapple for advantage. The winning move is to lift and carry your opponent for three consecutive steps. The big annual event is held each June in Edirne (north of Istanbul), but there are many smaller local events held throughout the country in summer. Camel wrestling (where two camels try to faze each other out – they rarely hurt each other) takes place in towns in the province of Aydın, including Selçuk, in December and January. For details of local events, inquire at the local Tourist Information Office in your resort. See **Yachting.**

Students: It is well worth taking an ISIC (International Student Identity Card) on a trip to Turkey. Substantial discounts are offered to students by Turkish Railways and Turkish Maritime Line. Many museums and archaeological sites also offer free entry or discounted admission fees.

Taxis: There are plenty of taxis in cities, towns and resorts. You can hail them in the street, pick them up at ranks in the town centre, or order by telephone (numbers can be found at hotels or Tourist Information Offices). Most taxis have meters. If there is no meter, ask to see the tariff card, which lists standard fares for various routes. Otherwise, it is up to you to settle a price with the driver before you get in. The cost of taxis is low compared to the UK; reckon on paying around £0.18 per km. See **Tipping.**

Telephones & Telegrams: Public telephones can be found at post offices, airports and railway stations. These use tokens called *jetons*, which come in three sizes: *küçük* (small) for local calls; *normal* (medium) for trunk calls within Turkey, cost 750TL; and *büyük* (large) for international calls, cost 2250TL. There are also cardphones which accept cards costing 8600TL and 17,100TL which may be more convenient for international calls. *Jetons* and phonecards can be bought at post offices; *jetons* are also available from stalls near public telephones. Look for the newer, yellow push-button phones, which have diagrams showing how to use them. These have slots for all three sizes of *jeton*.

Lift the receiver, insert a *jeton*, and listen for the continuous, high-pitched dialling tone. For a local call, just dial the number. For a long-distance call, dial 9, wait for the tone, then dial the area code then the number. For international calls (look for phones marked *Milletlerarası* – international), dial 9, and 9 again, then the country code (44 for UK, 1 for USA and Canada, 61 for Australia), then the area code minus the initial zero, then the number. When the little red light above the key-pad comes on, it's time to insert another jeton. The older black telephones are best for local calls only; dial first, then insert your *jeton* when your call is answered. Turkish cardphones work the same way as British ones. For the international operator, tel: 5282303.

Termessus: See ANTALYA-WALK, WHAT TO SEE, HISTORICAL SITES 2.

Time Difference: Turkish time is GMT plus two hours, all year round. This means that in summer it is one hour ahead of the UK.

Tipping: Restaurant and hotel bills usually include a service charge, but it is customary to tip the waiter around 5%. Tipping taxi drivers is not customary, but it is usual to round up the fare to the next 200TL. In a Turkish bath, it is normal to tip about 30% between the various members of staff. But if someone refuses a tip, do not force it on them, as this might offend.

Toilets: Public toilets can be found at bus stations, in restaurants, and in the vicinity of mosques. They are usually of the basic hole-in-the-ground variety, and flushed with a bucket of water filled from a tap in the wall. They are rarely supplied with toilet paper, so remember to bring your own. The plumbing was not designed to cope with wads of tissue, so place soiled paper in the bin provided. If there is an attendant, a small tip is in order. Toilets in most tourist pensions and hotels, however, are usually just like back home.

Tourist Information: The Turkish Ministry of Culture and Tourism operates Tourist Information Offices in towns throughout the region. They have lists of accommodation, and maps and leaflets describing

Marmaris

local attractions, and the friendly staff will do all they can to help with any enquiry you may have. You will find branches in Alanya, Antalya, Bergama, Bodrum, Çeşme, Dalaman Airport, Datça, Denizli, Fethiye, Foca, İzmir, Kaş, Kemer, Köyceğiz, Kuşadası, Manisa, Marmaris,

Pamukkale, Selçuk and Side. Before you leave home, you can get information from the Turkish Culture and Information Office, 170-3 Piccadilly, London W1V 9DD, tel: 071-7348681.

Tours: A number of companies offer coach tours of Turkey, generally of two to three weeks' duration, taking in Istanbul and all the main historic sights around the Aegean and Mediterranean coasts, finishing with a few days in one of the Mediterranean resorts. Package holiday companies offer more modest two-day coach tours from their resorts to major sights like Ephesus and Pamukkale. For more details, contact a travel agent, or check out a few package holiday brochures.

Transport: Public transport is relatively cheap, fairly easy to use, and very popular with the Turks themselves. The best way to get around the region by public transport is to use bus and dolmuş. The only rail service in the region is the express service between Ankara and İzmir, which takes about nine and a half hours. The train is generally slightly cheaper, and slower than the bus. Turkish Airlines (THY – *Türk Hava Yolları*) have regular internal flights connecting Istanbul and Ankara to İzmir, Antalya and Dalaman, which are relatively inexpensive (e.g. Istanbul to Antalya is about £55 one-way; students with ISIC can claim substantial discounts). However, internal flights are always busy, so book well in advance. Turkish Maritime Line runs a regular ferry service (cars and passengers) connecting Istanbul with İzmir, and from June-September there are 11-day cruises from Istanbul to Alanya and back, taking in most coastal towns on the way. These cost £300-600 all-in, including cabin, meals, day trips, etc. Again, book well in advance. There are numerous smaller ferry operators along the coast who run services between Bodrum, Datça and Marmaris, and from the Turkish mainland to the Greek islands of Chios, Samos, Kos and Rhodes. See **Buses, Dolmuş, Taxis**.

Traveller's Cheques: See **Money**.

Turkish Baths: The *hamam* is not the steam bath you might have expected, but simply a place to get clean. There are separate times for men and women – men generally in the morning and evening, women in the afternoon. You will be given a couple of towels and wooden bath-clogs (you can leave valuables in a locker at the desk), then shown to the changing room to undress. Wearing a towel, you will be shown to a cubicle in the steamy, marble wash room. Here buckets of hot water are poured over you, then one of the attendants will take a coarse cloth to your skin and rub you till you glow; you will be amazed at how much dirt comes off! You finish off with a rinse and a massage, before drying off and dressing again, feeling squeaky clean and on top of the world. See **Tipping**.

What's On: The best place to find out about coming events in your area is the local Tourist Information Office. In Bodrum and Marmaris you can buy magazine-type guides (*Bodrum and Environs: The Complete Guide*, and *Discover Marmaris*, 10,000TL each), published annually, that list local services and contain articles about local attractions. See **Events**, **Tourist Information**.

Yachting: Sailing holidays in Turkey are becoming increasingly popular, and are an ideal way to tour the beautiful Turkish coastline between Bodrum and Antalya. You can charter a yacht with an experienced skipper by the day or by the week, or join a flotilla holiday where a group of yachts cruise together, under the supervision of an experienced leader. Many package operators now offer holidays on *gulets*, lovely, Turkish-built wooden yachts that can accommodate 12 to 16 people in double cabins, and are designed for comfort rather than speed. They come complete with experienced skipper and crew, but it's up to you where he takes you. For further details of yachting holidays, ask at your local travel agent.

Youth Hostels: Because of the abundance of cheap pension accommodation, there is little demand for youth hostels in Turkey. The only one in the region covered by this book is in İzmir, and is intended mainly for Turkish students attending college. See **Accommodation**.